Friends
of Libraries
Sourcebook

EDITED BY

Sandy Dolnick

American Library Association

CHICAGO 1980

Table 1, "The Process of Management," is adapted from
"The Association Management Process: How to Practice
What We Preach," a resource of the Association of
Junior Leagues, Inc.

Figure 15, "Report Outline," is reproduced by permission
of the Brookfield, Wisconsin, Public Library.

Library of Congress Cataloging in Publication Data

Main entry under title:

Friends of libraries sourcebook.

   Bibliography: p.
   Includes index.
   1. Friends of the library—Handbooks, manuals, etc.
I. Dolnick, Sandy.
Z681.5.F78   021.7   80-24643
ISBN 0-8389-3245-2   1 Jul 81

Printed in the United States of America

083287

Contents

APPENDIXES

TABLE

FIGURES

Acknowledgments

In dealing with a project of this scope, it is impossible to list everyone who helped with its development and execution. I apologize for any names that have inadvertently been omitted.

I first want to thank the Friends organizations that responded to the survey and the Friends of Libraries Committee which has supported this work for many years. It is my hope that the results are worthy of the commitment made by its many members and past chairpersons.

Without the support of Donald Hammer, LAMA Executive Secretary during the development of the survey and book, the task could not have been completed. It would have failed without the help of Pearl Cohen, who helped with the large multiple mailings.

Karen Furlow, Sara Hite, Anne Mathews, Fran Donald, Joan Erwin, Barbara Healy, B. J. Jahnke, and Scott Bennett have been involved since the very beginning. I am especially grateful for the opportunity to work with such exceptional Friends, and for the fact that we remain friends. The American Library Association and its Publishing Services have been a joy to work with. I thank them for the opportunity to publish my experience as a Friend of the Library.

Sandy Dolnick

Introduction

Friends of Library organizations have changed both membership and direction in recent years. From groups of plump matrons chatting about literature and tweedy gentlemen with fat checkbooks, they have become citizen organizations that provide the library with money, numerous volunteer services, advocacy, public relations assistance, and community involvement. In today's world, Friends of the Library represent needed public participation in library affairs.

This sourcebook summarizes and expands on the results of a nationwide survey conducted by the Friends of Library Committee of the American Library Association. Seven-page questionnaires were mailed to more than seven hundred Friends groups chosen at random from the fifty states. Large, small, academic, and public libraries were surveyed. The Committee was pleased to receive a 46 percent response which is considered unusually good. The survey letter asked each Friends group to submit samples of the brochures, mailing pieces, and other printed materials that it uses. Many of these illustrate this book.

The Committee learned that every Friends organization, whether old or recently established, seeks new ideas. Everyone wishes to communicate on a broad scale, to discuss common problems, and to exchange ideas. This sourcebook, based on the typical committee structure of a Friends group, provides successful, proven examples of activities; it also examines the problems of a volunteer organization, since these too have to be considered for successful management. The ideas presented in this book can be used by academic or public libraries. They apply to both.

The contributors to this book have many different view-
points. Though they may reach identical conclusions, they
often do so by different routes. If a point is made several
times, remember it! That means it is important.

Grantsmanship and Internal Revenue Service and other federal forms are ignored in this book. These specialized matters are best treated by experts. The bibliography lists
sources for this information.

1. What's a Friend For

by

SANDY DOLNICK

with contributions by

Lillian M. Bradshaw

Hazel B. Maxwell

B. J. Jahnke

Elizabeth Mozley

Friends are a necessary part of life, for institutions as well as people. Support and recognition are important elements of any friendship. The basic assumption behind this book is that Friends of the Library groups can and should supply these necessities to all libraries while they represent the library to the community.

The potential effectiveness of a group of citizens with no vested interest cannot be overestimated. The library, which is often taken for granted, can multiply its support in the community if it is willing to establish and perpetuate a Friends organization.

Inflation and changes in public attitudes toward government spending have brought intense pressures to bear upon library budgets. In many cases, Friends of the Library, by raising funds from private sources or by providing volunteer labor, have made it possible to continue services that would otherwise have been terminated.

The initial reasons for having a support group differ among libraries and communities but generally include:

Money—Friends have traditionally raised funds for projects or acquisitions in excess of the general library budget.

Services—There is no limit to the services that a dedicated volunteer group can provide.

Public relations—Each Friend is a walking public relations vehicle for the library.

Advocacy—An informed, active citizen lobby can be the strongest weapon the library has.

Community involvement—An organized Friends group is living proof of the library's value to the community.

These subjects are covered in depth elsewhere in this book. It should be noted that the rationale for a Friends group may change over time. Groups that have begun as purely social organizations, for example, have shifted their orientation as the library's needs grew.

Friends of libraries, therefore, are many different things to many different communities. Basically they may be defined as groups of citizens that are associated on behalf of libraries.

The interest in Friends groups grows steadily. Every year the American Library Association receives more queries about them. Recently, Friends of Libraries USA, a national organization, was formed to further the growth of new groups and to exchange information among existing ones.

THE TEN COMMANDMENTS

Certain principles were discovered during the course of this study that many Friends groups had to learn by trial and error. Everyone works together more harmoniously if the Ten Commandments listed below are followed.

1. The library director must want a Friends group.
2. The library staff must be willing to work with Friends.
3. All parties involved in the organization of a group must realize the time commitment involved.
4. The library must agree which of its resources (e.g., space, staff time, paper, phones, etc.) will be used by the Friends.
5. A committed core group must exist.
6. The authority to which the library director reports (board of trustees; university provost) must be aware of the Friends group and must believe that it is needed.
7. Communication must be open to all groups involved in the use of the library; the Friends should not have an exclusionist policy.
8. All those involved must understand that Friends do not make policy.
9. The library must inform the Friends what role or roles they wish the organization to play: social, financial, educational, etc.
10. All those involved must understand that trustees and Friends have separate functions.

Groups should be able to check off each item listed as a group is being organized; an established group will find this list a good yearly evaluation. By renewing their goals each year, a group can retain the vitality of a new organization and reap the benefits of experience.

FRIENDS AND THE LIBRARY DIRECTOR

The relationship between the library director and Friends should be characterized by:

a basic understanding of goals and objectives
an appreciation of each other's individual potential for achievement
the shared enjoyment of ultimate success.

All parties must clearly understand their respective roles in order to work together toward common goals. The primary responsibility for bringing about this favorable state of affairs rests, in large measure, with the library director.

The library director must be prepared to respond to some fundamental questions and concerns relative to Friends. Among these are:

1. The director's desire for a Friends group and belief in the benefits of having such a group. Unless the library's leadership really wants a Friends group, it is less than fair to encourage citizens to form one.
2. Availability of time to work with Friends. Continuous communication, information, and encouragement are needed to sustain interest on the part of volunteers; the director must be available for such leadership.
3. Willingness to assist the Friends in understanding the legal and organizational structures of the library. If Friends are not told how they fit into the organization, chaos can result.
4. Necessary staff leadership in helping the Friends formulate long-term goals and short-term objectives. The Friends work program is most valuable when it moves the total library program forward. Groups should be challenged to think and plan on a broad scale.
5. Honest appraisals by both parties as to whether the library's program is worthy of a Friends group. If library programs do not meet community needs, a Friends group will be useless.
6. Time for attendance at all Friends meetings whether they be executive committee, board, or membership gatherings. The Friends must be made to feel that the library director is an important and indispensable part of their en-

deavors. This relationship should cultivate leadership by the Friends and not dependence on the director.

7. Praise and publicity for the achievements of the Friends. All appropriate governing bodies should learn of their achievements.

8. Awareness of how the community itself views the Friends. If the group becomes elitist, overspecialized, or simply social, it may antagonize voters in important library elections and bond campaigns. The director should see that Friends activities are broad-based and varied.

9. Most importantly, the realization that the work performance of the director can and should inspire faith in the library program and, therefore, increase and inspire the Friends' willingness to work for such programs.

Cooperation is vital. Without it, a library director can destroy a Friends group. On occasion, Friends have broken a library director. Understanding each other and working together, the library director and an effective Friends group can produce the most desirable of improved library services for the taxpayer and the user.

FRIENDS AND THE TRUSTEES

Library boards of trustees are created by law to act as the citizen control or governing body of the public library. The duties and responsibilities delegated to the board as a public trust are of two kinds: legal responsibilities enjoined upon the board by statute; and practical duties relating to the day-to-day operation of the library.

Except for the fiduciary and policy-making responsibilities assumed by trustees, the focus of Friends is identical to that of trustees—to assist the library in serving the entire community, recognizing the varying educational, recreational, and inspirational needs of all people. Friends, however, are so concerned with the quality and extension of library services that they organize independently for that purpose. Because Friends are entirely independent, they can often undertake projects that far exceed the scope of trustee or staff work. Friends can enrich the library's offerings and provide very special kinds of services. Because of their support and advocacy, Friends are often the library's most valuable resource.

Since Friends are so important, they should work in close partnership with the trustees. Communications remain open and mutual concerns are shared if trustees and Friends attend each others' meetings. Each organization should designate a special representative, and meeting agendas and minutes should be exchanged. Through experiences, trustees and Friends can work better toward their common goal of becoming invaluable advocates and interpreters of the importance of library service.

PITFALLS

There are times when the best intentions in the world have been frustrated; everyone is sorry that a Friends group was started. Following are some typical problems, described in quotations from Friends and librarians:

We are considered a fund-raising group by the library board and as an encumbrance by the director.

. . . on one hand we get the feeling we are not doing enough—and on the other that whenever we develop our own ideas, we are "overstepping."

Our director is very defensive and unsure of himself and refuses to let us communicate with the library trustees. He only wants to pull us out in a budget crisis.

The library staff is very supportive of us, but we have a weak director, and a public relations person who is jealous of our popularity in the town.

Anyone who has ever used a library on a regular basis seems to think he knows how to be a librarian.

The need for mutual respect between the Friends and the professional staff, director, or librarian is partly the librarian's responsibility too. The librarian's graduate work does not usually include training in the need to work well with laymen who are Friends and trustees.

The Friends need to recognize that the work in a library is never finished and yet, records must be kept and reports made to funding agencies at certain intervals, no matter what else is pressing. Friends should remember that personal time given for a Sunday afternoon program is a piece paid out of the librarian's life that cannot be recovered.

The majority of librarians are overworked and underpaid. Dealing with groups of people is time-consuming and can be nervously exhausting. Many librarians would prefer to be allowed to do the job without interruption.

Our librarian feels intimidated by our board of assertive community leaders who have been helping plan the expansion of our library.

How often does your Friends group recognize the extra
time the library staff has given you? If gratitude is
due, it should be given publicly.

Many of these problems could have been avoided—or easily
solved—if the Ten Commandments had been followed. Simple
courtesy, planning, and communication are the keys to success.

When professionals and laypeople work in an atmosphere
where authority is loosely defined, there will be some resent-
ment. Whether it is caused by an imagined slight or is simply
the neurotic reaction of a particular individual, the resent-
ment and resulting hostility are real to the people involved.
If a librarian begins to feel that a Friend threatens his or
her job, interferes with library work, or opposes policy, it
is time to find another place for the volunteer.

Few volunteers intend to provoke ill will. If there is a
personality conflict, however, it is the volunteer who must
adjust. Sometimes the problem can be overcome by changing as-
signments. It is also possible that some area of the library
will never be good for volunteers. If this is the case, they
should be removed completely. If difficulties persist, they
should be brought to the library director's attention. If no
help is forthcoming from that source, it is time to reassess
the situation.

Friends can be a valuable work force. They donate their
time, perhaps instead of money, to perform tasks that professionals cannot, because of time, money, or space limitations.

SERVICES PERFORMED BY FRIENDS

The primary purpose of a Friends organization is to be of
service to the library and to the community. Each library
and each community is different, with different needs and
different talents available. These needs can range widely,
from fund raising to lobbying for a local referendum, to providing snacks for the children in story hour. Each community
is unique and so, therefore, is each Friends organization.

The library director must work closely with the Friends
organization, especially with a newly formed group. The director must ensure that both have the same service goals in
mind; that adequate guidelines exist so that Friends can work
productively; and that Friends are adequately supervised.

The services that Friends organizations provide fall into
three broad groups: fund raising; service to the community;
and service to the library. Within these broad categories
there are jobs for those who wish to work with people, for
those with special talents, for those who like to work with

books, and for those who like to work with local, state, and federal governments.

These are some of the services performed by existing Friends organizations:

Services to the Community

Newsletter
Christmas open house
Produce and host televi-
    sion series or radio show
Book sales
Exhibit booth at county
    fair
Volunteers for the blind
High School essay contest
Parade float
Outreach program at re-
    tirement center
Film program for elderly
    in public housing
Oral history
Teachers' tea
Newcomers' Day
Survey on library use
Shut-ins brought to the
    library for National
    Library Week lunch, to
    meet staff, and the mayor
Send librarian to ALA
    Convention
Help for "mother's morning
    out"
Story-phone
Rare book appraisals
Dress pattern exchange

Service to the Library

Clerical help
Coffee and refreshments at
    programs
Decorate at Christmas
Tours of library
Clipping and setting up
    magazine file
Arrange displays
Manage grounds and shrubs
Painting
Shelving
Assist with mailings
Tune piano
Maintain Memorial Gift pro-
    cedure
Clip articles for vertical
    file
Free paperback book exchange
Typing
Mend books
Run library switchboard
Index newspapers
Index microfilm
Telephoning
Make bags to carry art repro-
    ductions

Purchases for the Library

Film programs
Special audiovisual equipment
Matching funds for Reading
    Is Fundamental grant
Books
Funds to increase endowment
Special furnishings
Rare books
Printing
Hospital book carts
Repair of rare books
Elevator for handicapped
Fiscal agent for Humanities
    Grant
Building repair
Security system
Rental book collection
Copy machine
Large print books
Landscaping
Shades
Rugs
Magazine subscriptions

One of the reasons why Friends organizations succeed is that many people are willing to work for a cause and accept recognition instead of a salary. A Friends organization can provide an opportunity for individuals to make a recognizable contribution to their community and to their own self-esteem. It provides an outlet for those who wish to be of service, for those who wish to polish job skills for re-entry into the working world, for retired citizens, and for the public's relations to the library. The librarian is using the community to help itself.

WORKING WITH VOLUNTEERS

Volunteers can be the library's most valuable asset. If they are treated with tact and intelligence, they will stay with the library and grow in usefulness. If not, they will find a place with another organization. Some general guidelines for working with volunteers are listed below.

Be precise in defining what you expect from the volunteer. You are entering into a verbal contract that may last for an hour or a year. It is only fair to tell volunteers what provisions have been made for them, how much work they are expected to accomplish, and how carefully it must be done.

Define the chain of command. Don't have too many chiefs and not enough workers. Whether a Friend or a library staff member is in charge, the volunteer should know whom to ask about particular problems.

Be sure adequate training is given. If the work involves library science, let a librarian do the orientation. Be sure that Friends understand how their tasks fit into the larger scheme of things.

Build in recognition. Appreciation of volunteers can be shown in a number of ways: teas, noting of their names in newsletters, certificates of appreciation, letters of recommendation, badges noting years of service, and personal notes. For people with limited incomes time is their donation; it should be recognized as much as a monetary one.

Build in some form of evaluation. This is as important to the library as it is to the organization. All points of view, including the public's, should be examined to find out if the service is valid, the volunteer capable, the time spent in proportion to the service given, and the expectations of all involved are being met.

This should be done periodically and on a continuing basis. It should be considered perfectly normal and not a threat to anyone.

Be hospitable.
Coffee, the use of the staff lounge, and a place for them to put their coats will make the Friends feel welcome. Providing a pleasant environment for a boring job can make volunteer hours more fun. When something special is being done, recognize it. Nice surroundings and people result in repeat visits from volunteers. Never assume that people know each others' names—provide name tags. Also, the tax benefits available to volunteers should be investigated. Mileage, parking fees, and other expenses related to volunteer work are often deductible.

Without volunteers, library services decrease. This may be suitable for some libraries that have volunteer services of their own, separate from the Friends, but for most, the variety of services that Friends can provide is a great asset and makes for a visible difference.

2. Getting Organized

by

BETTY THOLEN

ANN S. GWYN

KAREN LYNNE FURLOW

with contributions by

Barbara Healy

Scott Bennett

There is no special community group that is the natural starting point for formation of a Friends organization. Initial leadership can come from the library director who calls interested citizens together, or from an established organization. Groups who have assisted include: trustees, charity leagues, Rotary, Jaycees, American Association of University Women, Alumni, League of Women Voters, parent-teacher associations, faculty wives, Junior League, literary clubs, Federation of Women's Clubs. Someone must recognize the need for action and must provide enthusiastic leadership.

The situation is slightly different with university libraries. Long before there were Friends groups for these institutions, they had supporters who individually pursued a course similar to that of academic library Friends today. These people had a close personal interest in the library and its general growth and effectiveness. They contributed financially and in kind to the library's collections and articulated library needs and problems to others.

These early friends came either from the academic world or from the outside. They were the ones who provided an impetus to the formation of Friends groups. The earliest Friends organization was conceived by Archibald Coolidge, a Harvard University librarian, who worked with faculty and students to form an organization there in 1925. The Yale Library Associates were formed in 1930, following an eloquent plea to the alumni by Chauncey B. Tinker, an English professor. In other places, townspeople, business leaders, special donors, and bibliophiles have led the founding of academic Friends groups. Such memorable events as the presentation of a large donation or gift, receipt of the library's millionth volume, or the opening of a new library or wing have sometimes stimulated the founding of an academic Friends group. In every case, an important library official such as the director or the rare books librarian, has been involved. This person has provided leadership and has kept the Friends abreast of library needs, problems, and policies. No group is so broadly representative of an academic library's public as its Friends organization.

THE FIRST MEMBERS

If a Friends group is founded without the support of some existing community or academic organization, it is important that the first people chosen to speak for the Friends are representative of the types of people who will join. The entire tone of a Friends group is determined by its nucleus of organizers. If the founders are truly representative of the community, this is good. But the wrong person, even with the best of intentions, can wound or destroy a new organization. One librarian found out too late that the person she had entrusted with the job of building a Friends group was antagonizing both the community and her staff.

Well-known people should be encouraged to join the Friends. Even though they may have little time to give to the organization, their community contacts will be valuable. An attorney, to help with legal matters, and a person with publicity experience and media contacts should be recruited.

STEERING COMMITTEE

Once the decision has been made to form a Friends group, a steering committee or planning group should be established as soon as possible to maintain the initial enthusiasm. This committee should be representative of the library's constituency. Depending on circumstances, minorities or students should be invited to join. The committee will work in close consultation with the library leadership, the board of trustees, or the university administration, as appropriate.

FORMAL ORGANIZATION

The steering committee will probably decide to set up the Friends as a not-for-profit corporation. An attorney should be consulted about the procedures involved in doing so. (A

sample constitution is in the appendix.) Not-for-profit status
will enable the Friends to make mass mailings at third-class
rates and to file for tax exemptions. If granted, the exemption means the group pays no tax on its income (see chapter on
lobbying and legislation) and that contributions to the
Friends are income tax deductible. Virtually every religious,
charitable, and educational institution is a not-for-profit
corporation with tax-exempt status. It is extremely difficult
to raise funds for an organization that is not tax-exempt.

Before the Friends can incorporate, a constitution and bylaws must be written. These should state the name of the organization, the purpose, membership and dues structure, and officers and committees or boards and their respective duties.
The constitution and bylaws should also provide for meetings
and activities and should include procedures for amendment.

The constitution and bylaws should be short, concise, and
flexible enough to be functional as the organization grows and
expands. They should reflect long-range goals. A group that is
formed for the specific purpose of raising funds for a new library will find its task complete when the building is a reality. But since that is the time when volunteer citizens are
needed most to extend library services and to provide extra
support for new projects, the constitution and bylaws should
make long-term library support the goal of the organization
rather than a library building. The documents should be carefully phrased so that the Friends can obtain tax-exempt status
without delay. An attorney is best equipped to deal with these
matters. The library may have legal counsel or the Friends may
recruit an attorney who is willing to help.

All interested parties should review and comment on the constitution and bylaws. The steering committee may write a draft
and present it to the inaugural meeting of the Friends. Alternatively, the documents may be formulated at the inaugural
meeting. Drafts should be sent to the library leadership, the
board of trustees, or the university administration, as appropriate, before formal adoption by the membership. At Tulane
University, for example, the Friends steering committee wrote
a draft, sent it to the library and university administration
for review, and then presented an amended version to the inaugural meeting of the Friends.

After the Friends has been in operation for a year or so,
experience may indicate that the bylaws need to be amended.
The board may need to increase or decrease in size. Meeting
times may need to be changed or election procedures altered.
The bylaws are the means by which the Friends operate to reach
their goals. Guidelines for the group evolve through experience; each organization is different. It may well be several

years before the Friends have bylaws that are considered completely satisfactory.

Some groups have found that their constitution and bylaws
needed revision because they were cumbersome. Cornell University labored for years over a constitution. Once this docu-
ment was finally completed, it was so irrelevant and needless
that a copy could not be found.

Most groups have a president, vice-president, secretary,
and treasurer who performed the traditional duties associated
with these positions. Others have executive or advisory boards,
of ten to twenty-five members, which include the officers and
chairs of such committees as membership, program, publicity,
finance, and publications.

Student representatives sit on a number of executive boards
of academic groups. Almost all organizations include the library director or a representative as an ex-officio member of
the executive committee or advisory board. Dr. Powell of Duke
University states: "It's very inappropriate for the librarian
to be chairman . . . you have a selfish interest in it . . .
an organization such as the Friends would have more appeal and
would likely encourage more people to support it if its efforts are directed by someone not on the campus." Others have
said: "For the most part, holding office has been more an honorary than a working position"; "Library staff members should
not be officers! Friends should do the work instead of adding
to duties of short staffed libraries"; "It has been a problem
finding board members who would actually work."

A typical agenda for a board of directors meeting is presented below. For clarification on correct procedures for
handling various motions and discussions that occur, the chairperson should be familiar with parliamentary procedure. Even
in a small, informal group, adherence to the general etiquette
of parliamentary procedure will enhance the conduct of business and will satisfy all requirements for propriety.

Agenda

    Call to order
    Minutes of the previous meeting*
    Correspondence (may be read, summarized, or circulated)
    President's report (report on activities undertaken on be-
       half of group)
    Treasurer's report*
    Standing committees reports (e.g., volunteers, program,
       membership, publicity, or any committee that is part of
       the group's regular structure)
    Special committee reports (include such special efforts as

*motion called for

      fund-raising, book sales, receptions, National Library
      Week, et cetera)
Old business
New business
Adjournment*

*motion called for

PUBLICITY

With organizational questions out of the way, it is time
to tell the community about the Friends and to seek support
and membership. The news media are usually willing to use
their public service time and space on behalf of library activities and Friends groups. The Friends should do their home-
work first, however, if they expect cooperation. Editors are
best approached by a person who has publicity experience, media contacts, and a press release in hand. If the Friends desire free space or time for membership recruitment advertising, the ad should be prepared first and then submitted to the
appropriate person. Comments or suggestions from media professionals should be welcomed. If the organization wants to be
represented on a community radio or television program, it
should have available a list of knowledgeable speakers.

Many business firms and community organizations can provide valuable publicity support to Friends. Banks, fast food
restaurants, chambers of commerce, churches, and service clubs
may have bulletin boards, newsletters, or regular meetings
through which membership in Friends can be promoted.

CLARIFYING ROLES

Friends exist to help implement the policies of the trustees and library director. The group is free to function in
many ways as public relations agent and volunteer workers to
extend library services and information that could not be
handled by the regular staff. From the very start, therefore,
it is imperative that the library staff understand the purpose
of the Friends organization and accept it as an ally. Likewise,
members of the board of trustees or governing board should
know of the organization and should keep open channels of communication between the Friends and themselves. At no time
should actions of the Friends appear to infringe upon the
policy-making privileges of the trustees.

To facilitate cooperation, Friends should send a regular
observer or liaison person to trustee meetings. A trustee in
turn may be an ex officio member of the Friends board. As for

the library staff, the director is responsible for interpreting the activities of the Friends to the staff and for
enlisting their support and cooperation.

Building an active, growing Friends organization is often
a slow process. A noon film program, for example, may start
with a small group. If the first participants become involved
in film selection, however, and learn of other Friends activities, they will grow in numbers each year. Most beginnings
are modest. The used book sale may not raise as much money
in the first year as the one in the next town. The important
thing to remember at the beginning is that each activity
should make new Friends. As membership grows and the Friends
group becomes better known, its activities will gain more support. The ways that Friends can help to promote library services are limited only by the imagination of the membership.

GOALS AND OBJECTIVES OF ACADEMIC LIBRARIES

The results of the efforts of a Friends group are rarely
foreseen in the beginning, but in view of the large number of
libraries which have organized these groups, their worth has
been proven. It is the challenge of the Friends to generate
financial and other assistance to support further library development which is essential in building a good library. Some
of the most frequently listed goals of the academic Friends
group are:

1. To encourage gifts, endowments, and memorials to the library
2. To provide direct financial assistance by purchasing
   special and unusual items of great value which cannot
   be bought from the operating budget
3. To support special collections acquisitions activities
4. To support special fundraising programs for the library,
   such as building programs and collections in specialized
   subject areas
5. To stimulate community and campus awareness of the library
6. To sponsor programs designed to improve the cultural and
   intellectual life of the community and campus through
   lectures, programs, publications, and exhibits.

Though some Friends also list "advising the library administration" as one of their objectives, most seem content to contribute to the library in ways suggested by the library administration. Most notable is the National Women's Committee of
Brandeis University which has as its purpose "the support of
the library." This group funds over half of the total library
budget.

ADMINISTRATIVE ASSISTANCE

A paid employee of the Friends organization is a luxury reported by only a few university and public Friends groups. These, as may be expected, are the larger, more established groups. This person may be part-time or full-time, serving as executive secretary, keeping the financial and membership records, and carrying on the correspondence for the group.

Most often this work is done by library employees for academic groups; the office space, equipment, supplies, and labor are provided by the library. One respondent said: "In tax-supported institutions . . . the library staff gets stuck with most of the work and results are usually negligible or have no causal connection with Friends." The survey of Health Sciences Libraries Friends groups also showed that very few Friends groups have to perform their own secretarial work or to reimburse the library for such assistance.

HAZARDS

Survey respondents indicated that careful choice of leadership, judicious planning for the long term, and continuing review of the Friends goals and accomplishments are vitally necessary. "We had a 'false start' several years before actual organization," one respondent wrote. "We started with a 'committee' and the chairman didn't carry through . . . . The librarian and a board representative selected the beginning group. The first chairman or president *must* be dependable." Another stated that "our library director has placed his wife in charge of a very important project for our group. She has no organizational ability and refuses help when it is offered. It reflects on us, but we have no way out."

The bylaws should be written to provide for regular board turnover. Board members may have staggered terms and there should be a limit to the length of service allowed. The board should have representatives from all community groups. Members should vary in age, status, ethnic background, and education. If such provisions are not made, the board may become self-perpetuating. One respondent complained: "It has been my experience with the present group and with others, that after they have been established for many years, the active members tend to form a tight little unit that seems unwilling to make a concerted effort to get new blood into the organization. This situation can be very difficult to overcome!" Another declared that "I'm fairly new to the group, and I find a small group of long-time library supporters somewhat ingrown. New ideas and workers are welcomed but with reservations. A desire to retain the old tasks, friendships, relationships, etc., at the expense of attracting board members from a broader base in the community. Resistance to formal procedures and decision making is another problem."

Getting organized obviously takes a great deal more planning from the founders beyond the initial desire to start a Friends of the Library group. A knowledge of the community the group will serve is fundamental. Choosing leaders who will put the needs of the library above the personal needs of the committee is also valuable.

It is heartening to note the growing numbers of groups that have succeeded at this task, and the large number of aids designed to provide help in the formative period. These and further help, of course, are contained in subsequent chapters of this book.

It must be noted again that there is no one correct way to proceed, and if one method does not work, another will. The winning combination is those personalities and elements unique to each community.

3. Management by Objectives

by

SARAH C. HITE

Management by Objectives (MBO), a management system employed extensively and with success by corporations, government agencies, and libraries, can be used very effectively by Friends groups. While many Friends boards and their committees are undoubtedly doing most of the systematized straight thinking which MBO represents, the boards may not define as clearly their planned steps for efficient organization. Although MBO will not revolutionize Friends activities, it is a tool which, when used properly, can help a group define goals, evaluate accomplishments, and make plans. If Friends groups take the trouble to learn and apply MBO, hours will be saved. Like anything else, the more MBO is practiced, the easier it becomes.

DEFINITIONS

Several terms used in the MBO process are defined here. Table 1 depicts MBO in outline form.

MBO—Management by Objectives, a five-step cyclical management process.

Leadership—the *art* of getting people to do things. Leaders understand and make use of the motivations, needs, and emotions of others. Leaders find ways to get people to work with enthusiasm.

Management—the *science* of getting things done by use of five basic resources: money, manpower, materials, time, and authority.

Management process--an analytical system of organizing
resources to get results.
Purpose--the reason for being, why the group exists.
Goal--statement of intentions--general direction.
Objective--specific statement of what is to be accomplished
(or what will be different or changed) by what future
time and how results will be measured.
Method--plan; how to reach objectives.
Alternate plan--a contingency plan should the original fail.
Controls--a check, an assessment that warns of problems in
advance.
Evaluation--the first and/or final step. In the case of the
first step, a review of current resources and possible
directions. Review of results achieved, the use of resources, and the effectiveness of management.

THE STEPS

Evaluation

This is the beginning and ending step of MBO, something the
Friends board and each committee should do at the beginning of
each new officer's term. The board should ask itself: What are
our present achievements? Where do the Friends want to go?
What do we think is important? What volunteers, money, materials, time do we have available? What do our members want? What
needs to be done? What can we do? These and other questions
need to be answered before a group can set objectives. A group
has to know its philosophy and its abilities *before* beginning
its work.

Goals and Objectives

A Friends group should first have its purpose firmly in
mind, the reason for its existence. Basically, the task is to
assist the library, to help provide good library service to
the community. What then are the goals and the general operating direction? These are probably stated in the bylaws and
should be examined occasionally to see if they are still timely. Possible goals might be:

To promote the library in the community
To sponsor community events and activities
To provide special items for the library
To encourage gifts, endowments, and memorials
To promote volunteer activities
To raise funds
To act as an advocate

TABLE 1. The Process of Management

PURPOSE: the mission that the organization is intended to fulfill

GOAL: a general aim implied by the mission

OBJECTIVE: a measurable outcome which makes the goal operable

MANAGEMENT PROCESS (Management by Objectives)

--a systematic way of organizing resources to get something done

--a five-step cyclical process

1. DEFINE and COMMUNICATE OBJECTIVE(s)

2. ORGANIZE FOR ACTION:

      a. develop and define concept (how are we going to do this)
      b. allocate resources
            money
            manpower
            materials
            time
            authority
      c. alternate plans

3. CONTROLS: Sensing devices to warn of impending failure

      a. feedback
      b. timetable
      c. observation

4. EXECUTION: Carry out plans

5. APPRAISAL: Systematic evaluation with the following in mind:

   a. did we or did we not meet our objectives?

   b. how were resources used?

   c. how well did we manage?

   d. as a result of this appraisal, what recommendations about future goals and objectives might we make?

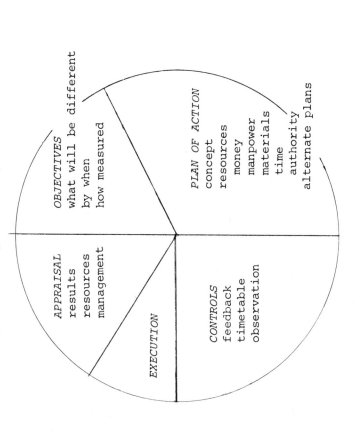

OBJECTIVES
what will be different
by when
how measured

PLAN OF ACTION
concept
resources
money
manpower
materials
time
authority
alternate plans

APPRAISAL
results
resources
management

CONTROLS
feedback
timetable
observation

EXECUTION

To inform the community about programs, activities, resources, and needs.

These goals are very general statements of intent, things
a group would like to see come about. Accomplishment of some
or all of these goals demonstrates that a Friends group is
meeting its purpose.

However, the most difficult job in management is translat-
ing goals into defined and specific objectives before initi-
ating, planning, or tackling a task. Objectives not only state
what is to be accomplished, they also define *by when* and *how
measured.* By establishing specific objectives at the beginning
of new officers' yearly terms, the Friends board knows what
it is trying to do: decisions, policies, and priorities can
then be made in view of this. Loosely organized Friends boards
and committees often try to follow *general* goals. Conversely,
boards and committees who set and follow specific objectives
are generally well-organized, operate with a minimum of lost
or wasted effort and resources, and develop a high esprit de
corps because they know their goals and can later measure
their achievements. Following are some examples of objectives
a Friends organization might establish after first making a
self-appraisal and deciding upon some general goals:

Goal: To raise money for the library.

Objective: To have a used book sale by June of next year
that will raise $3,000.

Goal: To provide programs in the library.

Objective: To sponsor four programs on "How the West Was
Won." These will be held on the first Thursday in September, November, January, and March with an average
attendance of 100 people.

Goal: To increase the membership of Friends.

Objective: To increase membership by 200 before December 30.

Goal: To have an annual meeting

Objective: To invite a well-known author for a dinner
meeting on March 3 which 200 people will attend.

Goal: To act as an advocate for the library.

Objective: To increase City Council funding for the library by 6 percent, including funds for new programs.

Each of these objectives tells what changes will occur,

tells when the objective is to be reached, and includes a
standard of measurement. Once the objectives have been determined by the board and assigned to a committee, the group is
ready for the next step.

Organizing for Action

How will objectives be accomplished? What is the plan? How
will it be made to happen? Available are the five resources
available to every manager, and therefore planning is essen-
tially the allocation of these: people, money, material, time
and authority. Following are some questions which need to be
asked about each.

In terms of people, how many are needed? Who will select
them? Who will do what? What training is necessary?

How much money is there? How much is really needed to do
the job? Where could more be obtained if necessary? Are there
cuts that could be made?

What materials are needed? How will they be selected, allocated, produced?

How much time is there? How much is needed? Is there a reserve? Is there a critical time path on which the plan hinges
or a series of deadlines?

How shall authority be delegated? How many restraints
should be put on the committee waiting for board approval?

For any objective there obviously can be several approaches
for bringing about the desired result. Each approach dictates
a different mix in the allocation of the five resources. Planning requires that the Friends organization assess all its resources and capabilities and then draw up a plan which takes
maximum advantage of these. One thing to remember in allocating resources, however, is to keep some in reserve. *Don't allo-
cate all resources: there may be an emergency or the need to
strengthen some portion of a plan.*

Considering Alternate Plans

This is the final step in planning. Wrong assumptions, un-
known factors, or simply a change in circumstances might call
for a change in plans. To the extent that these can be thought
out ahead and instead of committing much time and energy to
worrying about what might go wrong, a Friends group should
have an alternate plan. What if the guest speaker cannot make
it at the last moment? What if the outdoor event is rained out?

Planning, then, might be defined as simply trying to project the experiences that the group will eventually have. Experienced people can obviously better anticipate certain like-

lihoods and the most effective planners will be those who discipline themselves to think through, step by step, future situations. Such people also consider the possibilities for failure and plan accordingly.

CONTROLS

Successful managers not only consider what might go wrong, but establish warning systems that tell them *in time* so they can take action at once. If the manager becomes aware that things are not going well during the course of a project, corrections can be made early. Conventional controls are budget, time, costs, and written or oral reports. If a budget has been made and costs are excessive, the manager must take action. Serious deviations from schedule are another warning.

Progress reports give the group a sense of direction, and tell everyone how things are progressing. Other controls include:

Standards of Performance

Everyone should know what is expected of everyone else. This should be established before the committee or group starts to work and should be accepted by all. This offers a standard to determine if each person is doing his or her job.

Personal Observation of the Manager

The more the manager can observe the situation personally, the more easily adjustments can be made in the plan.

Feedback

In addition to the manager's observation, the evaluation of others is important. This is done informally. The manager may ask participants: How do you feel things are going? How do you think plans are shaping up?

Control systems can be very expensive in time, effort, and in the negative atmosphere they sometimes engender. Hence, the simpler the controls, the better--as long as they work!

EXECUTION

In executing the plan, the manager or the board steps back and watches events take their course. The hardest part of this step is to let people who have been assigned jobs do them without interference. The key to effective execution is experienced

and motivated people. This is where leadership really counts.
Courage, commitment, and dedication make the difference.

EVALUATION

Evaluation is the final step. As mentioned earlier, Management by Objectives is a cyclical process which returns to the
point where it started. Evaluation as the final step has three
parts.

First, were the objectives achieved? Subobjectives, such as
meeting membership needs, should also be evaluated. Were resources used effectively? Did the group overcommit its money?
Were volunteers undercommitted? What was the cost in time ver-
sus the return? Were the results worth the effort and use of
resources? Was the management process followed? In any part of
this appraisal, it is very important to list both positive
and negative results.

Second, where do the Friends go from here? This is an internal appraisal, looking again at the Friends resources and
policies and how to use them.

Third, how were the library and the community affected? Was
the project important to them? Are the Friends fulfilling a
real need in the library and the community?

The final portion of the evaluation process is to coordinate the Friends assets and capabilities with the needs of the
library and the community. The Friends should determine what
they can do best that will help the library the most. New
goals and objectives can then be set for the next year. Each
board should write a set of objectives and plans for its successors for the forthcoming year. Though the new board may
accept, modify, or create its own objectives, it should be
able to get underway quickly and continue on a successful
course.

Some people are concerned that if management is approached
as a science and as a defined process, individuality and personal flair will be stifled. This is not true. Within a defined framework, Friends groups can be creative, innovative,
and challenged. Everyone will know and understand where the
organization committee is going, how it plans to get there,
and what is required. MBO does not replace or displace imagination or good judgment. It is simply an organized way of
doing things which, when followed, will insure the continuity
of the Friends operations, insure directed activities, and
provide a framework for progress.

4. Membership Recruitment

by

FRANCES G. DONALD

with contributions by

Karen Lynne Furlow

Ann S. Gwyn

Scott Bennett

Cecil T. Young

This chapter gives suggestions for promotion and recruitment of membership in Friends groups for public libraries, summarizing the experience of Friends organizations nationwide and providing many samples of successful promotional materials. The chapter also gives guidelines for obtaining new members for Friends of an academic library and describes solicitation of corporate memberships.

The rules are not hard and fast; in fact it is constantly amazing how inventive means are initiated by dedicated volunteer library lovers to promote and recruit Friends of the Library. It is not like climbing Mount Everest: There's a great well of good will out there toward libraries, just waiting to be tapped. We like the comment of one chairperson who answered the question, "What incentives do you have for membership?" with "Love of the library is incentive in and of itself."

THE BASIC TOOL

Never underestimate the value of word of mouth in interesting people to join the Friends of the Library, but at some point it is necessary to decide that you have to communicate with a wider audience; to support the printed word you will have to get into it yourself.

It may be a simple, friendly letter, such as figure 1, or a professionally designed and printed brochure (figures 2 and 3). Whatever the budget allows, the following information should be provided for prospective members:

THIS YEAR, MORE THAN EVER -
WE NEED FRIENDS TO STRENGTHEN
THE LIBRARY'S RESOURCES!

THE FRIENDS OF THE EASTCHESTER PUBLIC LIBRARY are beginning a new season.

As a FRIEND, you are part of a growing non-profit volunteer citizens group
believing in the importance of books, cultural activities, and libraries
for people of all ages.

In past years, the FRIENDS have - to name only a few of their accomplishments -
purchased the initial collection of framed art reproductions for circulation,
sponsored and/or co-sponsored many important Film Series, lectures on a variety
of subjects, art shows, musical programs, craft exhibits, purchased the 16mm
sound projectors and screen, jointly purchased with the Library the Offset
Printing Machine, and have yearly supported and expanded the scope of library
services and activities that would not have been available with only the
library budget.

This season, the FRIENDS hope to provide a change machine for the convenience
of the many patrons who use the copy machines. Other plans include increasing
the number of circulating games, book related events, and guest speaker
appearances.

With the support of people like you, it is possible for us to execute these
plans and invite all people to make fuller use of the opportunities and
services the Library offers.

WON'T YOU BE A FRIEND? Please use the enclosed envelope, and add any
comments you may have.

RAE WEISBECKER   - PRESIDENT
THOMAS PALMER   - VICE PRESIDENT
ROSE PALLADINO   - TREASURER
FRAN MURRAY   - SECRETARY
HARVIA RUSSELL   - MEMBERSHIP

Fig. 1. Publicity for membership promotion--Friends of
Eastchester Public Library

Fig. 2.   Publicity for membership promotion--Friends of the
          Greenwich Public Library

¹friend \'frend\ n [ME frend, fr. OE frēond; akin to OHG friunt
friend; both fr. the prp. of a prehistoric Gmc verb represented by
OE frēon to love; akin to OE frēo free] 1 a : **one attached to an-**
other by affection or esteem b : ACQUAINTANCE 2 a : one not
hostile b : one that is of the same nation or group 3 : one that
favors something 4 obs : PARAMOUR 5 cap : a member of a group
that stress Inner Light, reject ostentation, outward rites, and an
ordained ministry, and oppose war — called also Quaker
²friend vt : to act as the friend of : BEFRIEND

Everyone Needs a Friend .....

..... Including The Richmond Public Library

Fig. 3.   Publicity for membership promotion--Friends of the
          Richmond Public Library

Goals

You can be general (like Wabasha, figure 4) or specific
(like Clearwater, figure 5). Perhaps the director of your library has a project that cannot be provided in a year of bud-
get-crunch. In any case, you should discuss and clear the
draft with your librarian, so you will both know what the
Friends are and where they are heading.

Incentives for Membership

The majority of Friends offer a wide range of incentives:
they provide opportunities for volunteer work in the library
or interesting activities in which members can participate;
they send out monthly calendars or newsletters, special invitations to events, programs, and exhibit openings; they offer
discounts, and sometimes free gifts at book sales (figure 6).
Remember also that one important incentive for membership in
all nonprofit Friends groups is that dues are tax-deductible.

The Fee Schedule

Since love of libraries crosses all economic barriers, most
Friends groups have a graduated dues schedule. Members give as
little as a dollar, or as much as a thousand dollars. Some
groups have a special schedule for business and corporations;
these are described at the end of this chapter, and an example
of a combined fee schedule is shown in figure 7.
The schedule is almost invariably printed on the blank
which is a part of the printed piece, so the new member can
check off a category of contribution. A good many Friends
groups print the fee schedule and membership blank on the re-
verse side of an envelope which can then be mailed with the
contribution back to the library.

Questionnaires and Surveys

If one of your goals is to get volunteers to devote time
and energy to the library, you may decide to combine a membership appeal with a questionnaire for prospective workers to
fill out in order to make full use of their talents. Perhaps
a survey of activities, events, or services the respondent
would like to see in the library would be helpful to the library administration as well as the Friends.

HOW TO REACH PROSPECTIVE MEMBERS

Dropping leaflets from a balloon was about the only method

Be a friend.

Friends of the Library is just that simple.

It's people who take books to the hospital and nursing home. It's people who help with used book sales, serve coffee at library events and do some other odds and ends.

The Friends aren't too big on organization. Someday, perhaps, there will be dues and bylaws and such. But for now, anyone who drops by a meeting and is willing to participate is welcome. They each put a buck on the cookie plate once last year, if you want to call that dues.

That's not to say the group doesn't have plans for the future. The first annual art fair in the park (Fall of 1975) was a Friends project. And adult classes in cross-country skiing, needlework and photography that winter was another. The Friends try to do some of the things nobody else is doing in Wabasha.

If being a Friend appeals to you...if you have interests in the sorts of things a public library might be involved in...ask the librarian when the next meeting will take place.

There's an extra cookie on the plate...for you.

Friends of the Library

Wabasha Public Library
168 Allegheny Avenue
Wabasha, Minnesota 55981

Fig. 4. Publicity for membership promotion--Friends of the Library, Wabasha Public Library

Fig. 5. Publicity for membership promotion--Friends of the Clearwater Public Library

BEST SELLERS DRAWING NO. ——

The Friends are giving away the following best sellers as part of the festivities celebrating the election of new officers and the conclusion of another year's annual meeting.

The Ascent of Man by Dr. J. Bronowski, Little, Brown, $17.50: Beautifully produced collection of lectures on the rise of science as originally aired on PBS.

Ragtime by E. L. Doctorow, Random House, $8.95: "The raggedy music of turn-of-the-century America...with darker bass notes."

...erzy Kosinski, Houghton, $8.95: The latest ...he Painted Bird. Intrigue, violence and ...n, Random House, $7.95: anthology of some ...VEN AWAY.

An Invitation

Established October 8, 1857

FRIENDS *OF THE* SACRAMENTO PUBLIC LIBRARY

Fig. 6.   Publicity for membership promotion—Friends of the Sacramento Public Library

FRIENDS OF THE
DETROIT PUBLIC LIBRARY, INC.

1977 CORPORATE & PROFESSIONAL
MEMBERSHIP DRIVE

DUES CATEGORIES

Major Sponsor $5,000

Sponsor $2,500

Associate Sponsor $1,000

Sustaining Sponsor $500

Affiliate Sponsor $250

Patron $100

Member $50

Additional information about the Friends of the Library may be obtained by calling 833-4048. Inquiries about special contributions should be directed to the Development Office (833-9768).

PHILIP G. MOON, *Chairman*
Corporate & Professional Campaign

PAUL T. SCUPHOLM, *Executive Secretary*

*   *   *   *   *

The Friends of the Detroit Public Library, Inc., is a not-for-profit, 501(c)3 charitable foundation located at 5201 Woodward Avenue, Detroit, Michigan 48202. It is registered with the State of Michigan, Department of Attorney General, as MISC 5886.
7713F

WJBK-TV ● Hiram Walker & Sons, Inc. ● Wayne Oakland Bank ● Whitehead & Kales Co. ● David M. Whitney Fund ● Willey Foundation ● Williams Research Corporation ● Winkelman's ● Woodall Industries, Inc. ● Woodlawn Cemetery Association ● Xerox University Microfilms.

Fig. 7. List of dues categories--Friends of the Detroit Public Library, Inc.

not reported by Friends groups as a way of appealing for membership in the community. Actually, we would not want to bet that some enterprising group has not tried that. Here are some successful efforts as reported in the survey:

Bookmarks

Since the most likely prospects are library users, a bookmark slipped into books checked out by each patron is certainly an on-target method of promotion, acting as a gentle reminder while the book is being read. The bookmark has the added advantage of being economical, requiring no postage and little paper, although the Houston Public Library added a nice touch by including a tear-off membership blank which could be mailed back free (figure 8). In most cases, the prospects are expected to fill out the blank and turn it in with their books. The bookmark's one disadvantage is that any message needs to be very concise.

Mailing

Obviously, you will need a budget for postage charges: large mailings are expensive. Once a mailing list tops two hundred, you will be eligible for bulk mail, which brings the cost down considerably. As of this writing, however, the bulk-mail regulations are being revised, so it is wise to obtain the latest information. Briefly, you will be required to purchase a post office number, which will be printed on the envelope in place of a stamp. If your library already has a bulk-mail account and number, you may be able to use that. Bulk-mail costs are lower because envelopes or mailers are presorted into bundles by zip code before they are taken to the post office. Each piece in the mailing must be exactly the same in size and weight.

As your organization grows in membership, you might consider budgeting for an addresser-printer to save volunteer time in endless hand-addressing.

Another saving, both in cost of envelopes and the time required to stuff them, will be accomplished if your brochure or flyer is a "self-mailer," leaving space on one panel for the address (figure 9).

Finding the names of prospects can be helped immeasurably by loans of member lists from such organizations as the League of Women Voters, the Chamber of Commerce, service organizations, or alumni groups. Several Friends brochures provide the space for new members to suggest other names. Here's a method reported from a Friends group in Pennsylvania:

This year we are sending invitations to all library

Fig. 8.   Publicity for membership promotion--Friends of the
          Houston Public Library

Friends of the Kenosha Public Library

Membership Application

Name:

Address:

Telephone number:

_____ Individual Annual Membership
$1.00

_____ Individual Annual Supporting
$5.00

_____ Organizational Annual Membership
$10.00

_____ Life Membership
$100.00

**Memberships are renewable in April
of each year.**

Fig. 9. Publicity for membership promotion--Friends of the Kenosha Public Library

patrons (35,000) . . . we plan to at least triple our membership. Using the registration files is like getting a specialized zip code marketing plan . . . a gold mine.

Almost any available list will include some library lovers.

If your budget for postage is not as large as you would like, do not worry. The Friends of the Bell Public Library in Portland, Texas, got the Boy Scouts to deliver their appeal door-to-door; and the Friends of the Emporia Public Library designed their brochure as a tent card which they placed in restaurants, thus giving diners food for thought as well. The Welcome Wagon will often loyally put your information in the hands of new residents.

Newspapers, Radio, and Television

You should coordinate your membership drive with releases in the local newspaper, announcements on the local radio station, and even television, if access is possible. Library promotion on radio and television is usually welcomed since it helps to fill the station's public service requirement. Your local newspaper editor might be delighted to write an editorial for you—there is little risk in being horsewhipped by an irate citizen for supporting the library.

If your Friends group is already a going concern, reports of its activities or sponsored events in the newspaper throughout the year help you with recognition when it comes time for your membership drive; if you're just organizing, perhaps you should urge your group to start off with something newsworthy, such as a first annual picnic, or bringing a circus to town, or an elegant Open House at the library.

You can also go piggyback with national advertising and publicity about libraries during National Library Week by making your membership year April to April. If your budget can be stretched, paid advertisements or spot announcements can be enormously helpful.

One caveat on all Friends publicity: clear it and time it with your library director. Coordination is supportive; competition is not.

Posters

If someone in your group is a graphic artist, then posters make a nice complement to a membership drive. They should not be regarded as a prime source for getting new members, however, since they require the prospective member to get the blank, fill it out, and mail or take it to the library. Therefore, if posters are included in your publicity scheme, make sure they are around the entire library and are accompanied by membership blanks.

ACKNOWLEDGMENT OF MEMBERS

Some Friends groups have little wallet cards printed up to issue to new members; some send out a welcoming, grateful letter (figures 10 and 11). You may decide a telephone call would be even better. In any case, make new members feel welcome.

CONTACT AND EVALUATION

Work each year will be made easier if you keep in touch with members throughout the year, with information about the library in a newsletter, or invitations to special events and programs, or recognition of volunteers in the newspaper, or all of these. At the very least, each member should receive an annual report of your activities.

Furthermore, take a tip from your librarians, past masters in the art, and keep meticulous records of both the "do'ers" and the "don'ters." The latter may think better of it next year.

Indeed, a periodic evaluation of your Friends membership can often point up a target area that is rife with possible members. Look at the spread geographically: is it all concentrated in one section of town? Or economically: is it lopsided in upper middles or lower uppers? Or ethnically, or any other way you can think of. If you see an unrepresented area, try a personal call to a community leader. You'll be surprised how that kind of appeal can achieve a continuing neighborhood of library supporters.

When eminent historian Barbara Tuchman was asked for a quote for the Friends of the Greenwich Library's membership brochure (figure 2), this is what she wrote: "Friendship for libraries is enlightened self-interest." That should serve as the last word.

RECRUITING FRIENDS FOR AN ACADEMIC LIBRARY

The typical university Friends group has between 250 and 500 members. A number of the larger and more wealthy institutions report over 1,000 members. There seems to be no relationship between the size of the university and the size of the Friends.

Faculty and alumni comprise the largest percentage of the membership: the remainder is made up of students, book collectors, and other community people. One respondent remarked, "there are very few wealthy book collectors in our area . . . so the Friends are made up of faculty and staff. This does not make for a strong and effective organization." Another

Fig. 10. Membership cards for Friends groups

FRIENDS OF THE CLEVELAND PUBLIC LIBRARY, INC.

325 SUPERIOR AVENUE   ·   CLEVELAND, OHIO 44114   ·   623-2821

Dear Friend:

   Welcome to membership in the Friends of the Cleveland
Public Library. Your new membership card is enclosed. Just
a reminder - your membership is tax deductible on next year's
income tax return.

   We appreciate your interest. It is through membership
contributions such as yours that we are able to provide much
needed support for the important work of the Cleveland Public
Library - the downtown Main Library, as well as the 35 branches
throughout Greater Cleveland.

   Enclosed you will find a coupon which entitles you to a
$2.50 discount on the purchase of a new book at the listed book
stores. You will be receiving regular copies of the *Friends'
Newsletter* and *Marginal Notes*.

   Your ideas and suggestions for the Friends' organization
are always most welcome, but especially at this time when we
are reviewing and reorganizing many of our activities. Won't
you take a few minutes and stop by our office on the fourth
floor of the Main Library the next time you're downtown to
become better acquainted? Or you can feel free to call us at
any time - 623-2821. We want to hear from you.

   Good wishes.

                                    Sincerely,

                                    Ella Mae Howey

                                    Ella Mae Howey
                                    Executive Director

EMH:nd
Enclosures

Fig. 11.   Letter of welcome to members of Friends of the
           Cleveland Public Library, Inc.

commented, "as our older benefactors die it seems increasingly
difficult to identify younger alumni who are both bibliophiles
and generous donors." It takes a long time to build up in the
Friends a sense of pride that results from free and generous
contributions of money, manuscripts, and books to a library
with which they can identify.

TARGETS AND TECHNIQUES

Alumni groups and university faculty are the obvious first
groups from which to start recruiting. These people most likely have a common interest in the library already. At very
large schools, it may be most fruitful to concentrate on the
faculty and graduates of the humanities and other areas that
depend heavily on the library. Friends may focus on those who
have earned specific kinds of degrees. A great deal will depend on how alumni records are organized at the university. If
the school is in an urban area, the general public may be approached.

As the Friends grow, they will enter what might be called a
second phase of development, in which their simple existence
will attract support that would otherwise be lost. A channel
for giving, once opened, will be used—though perhaps not
filled. Such an arrangement can become largely passive, however, and dependent on a minimal public relations effort to
keep people interested in and attracted to the library.

Referral—when members themselves start to recruit new members—is a third, very desirable, phase of development. This
happens when the Friends take up a place in the social life of
their members and when the group benefits from their volunteer
activity. At times, this activity will have no connection with
either the university or, initially, the library. At this
point, the Friends' public relations must address a wide spectrum of interests. The library is in some measure dissociated
from its institutional parent and becomes a focus of concern
in its own right. In this way, Friends membership becomes self-
generating and self-renewing.

INCENTIVES TO JOIN

Prospective members usually receive an attractively designed packet of information about the Friends group, which
may include an application for membership, a brief statement
of the purposes and objectives of the group, and a description
of its accomplishments.

All Friends groups attempt to communicate with their members on a regular basis. This may be done through a simple

letter that announces an upcoming meeting or event, or through a scholarly journal, issued twice or three times a year, such as *Columbia Library Columns, Books at Brown,* or *Library Notes* (Duke University). A few libraries offer the use of the library and the services of its professional staff, including checkout privileges.

Persons who give large sums may have their names printed in the Friends publication; noteworthy gifts and donations are often reported there. The Friends group itself may sponsor and support additional publications for the library such as guides or inventories of special collections, library handbooks, and brochures and programs for lectures and meetings of the group.

"Keepsake" volumes, or yearly gifts may be issued to those at special levels of membership. These are usually reprints of rare works owned by the library. The Cornell University Friends group reprinted a popular murder mystery set owned by the library and offered a copy to everyone who donated $25 or more to the Library Associates. This more than doubled the number of persons giving at that level. The Cornell Library Associates reports that it always has something to distribute, ranging from handsome printings of original poetry to illustrated brochures advertising talks and exhibits.

For exceptional gifts or collections, specially designed bookplates may be prepared, a section or shelf of the library may display a plaque with the donor's name, or a room or wing to house a significant collection may be built to pay tribute to the benefactor. All gifts must be acknowledged, however. The word of thanks may come from the Friends group, the rare book librarian, the university librarian, or even the president of the university.

MEMBERSHIP CATEGORIES AND FEES

Four or five categories of membership are listed by most academic groups, with quite a variety of titles, in an attempt to attract members at all levels. About 40 percent of the university library Friends groups report a student rate. Florida State University, Louisiana State University, University of North Carolina at Chapel Hill, Texas A & M University, and University of Wisconsin charge only two dollars for a student membership; the University of Massachusetts and the University of Missouri at Kansas City have a three dollar student fee; and at least ten other Friends groups charge students only five dollars. Except for those mentioned above, the student category of membership, the least expensive, was about ten dollars. At the other extreme, most Friends groups have a "life" or "benefactor" membership category, for which $1 thousand or even $5 thousand or the equivalent gift is contributed.

A few Friends groups have only one classification of membership. For example, one may become a member of the Yale Library Associates for only twenty-five dollars, or an equivalent gift. The Yale Library Associates presently has over eight hundred members. The Friends groups at Dartmouth College and Miami University (Ohio) are supported entirely by voluntary contributions.

CORPORATE MEMBERSHIPS

In order to achieve maximum influence, Friends should be aware of two important points. First, the financial and moral support of the corporate community is vital if the Friends group is to grow beyond an ad hoc volunteer group. It is of course possible to finance Friends through memberships, book sales, benefits, and the like. But successful nonprofit organizations, such as museums and orchestras, all have a solid base of corporate support.

Second, every possible channel of communication must be used to make the business community aware of the role and the needs of Friends. Business will respond if approached correctly. Support from certain segments of this community may depend upon the degree to which Friends are perceived as a valuable cultural resource. Potential supporters may be interested in activities that make library services available to the poor and the handicapped. Corporate contributions policies may advocate support of such projects as making library discards available at a nominal price and delivery of books to the disabled and homebound.

Friends should think carefully about the nature and type of support desired from business. The Friends may seek funding from a few firms for special projects. Another approach is to develop categories of membership for corporations that will attract substantial annual contributions toward ongoing operating support. The business membership fee schedule should contain a range that allows small and large firms to participate. The different member categories can be designated as patron, sponsor, benefactor, and the like.

Business firms will be most receptive to a logical appeal that is put into writing. They should be told what the Friends organization does, why it needs money, and how gifts to the Friends will benefit the community. Putting this into writing requires much thought, time, and effort but is a necessary prerequisite to corporate support.

The rationale summarized below was successfully used by one Friends group to train persons who solicit corporate and foundation contributions. The general approach of this organization can be adapted to fit the requirements of almost any Friends group.

1. The library is a basic educational resource for all citizens. It is of increasing importance since people need more and more information to cope with the complexities of urban society.
2. As a public agency, with its income derived primarily from local property taxes, the library is chronically short of the funds that are needed to maintain high standards of community service.
3. Inflation has caused costs to outpace revenues, resulting in a gradual erosion of services with fewer books, shorter hours, and a smaller staff.
4. Friends help the public library to maintain and improve its services by supplementing tax appropriations with private funds and by providing volunteer labor.
5. As the volunteer arm of the library, the Friends have been increasing their contributions. As budgets tighten, the needs of the library and the Friends will increase.
6. The Friends have been building the financial and organizational base that will enable them to meet the growing needs for library support services.
7. The most important need of the Friends is to coordinate their volunteer activity through a full-time paid director and office staff. At present, the Friends have only part-time people.
8. The Friends take primary responsibility for library-based cultural activities. Programs relating to books and authors, manuscripts, rare books, and special collections can most logically be carried out by Friends in cooperation with the library administration.
9. Over the past few years, many business firms have become annual members of the Friends, providing funds for improvement of office operations and programs.
10. Membership categories have been established at annual rates of $25, $50, and $100. Several firms have contributed additional sums, the highest being $1,000. The Friends hope to increase their supporting membership while inviting higher contributions.

Friends should plan to solicit at least 50 percent of their membership income from the business community. Several organizations have already achieved this objective. It follows from this that the business community is an important library constituency. Business participation in Friends must be accompanied by recognition that the business community has great needs for library and information services; the library should meet these to the best of its ability.

As a general rule, business people, like other members of the public, do not know of the many resources that the li-

brary has available for them. Therefore, a long-range informational program designed for the business community should be
developed as a basis for future financial support. It is important that corporate Friends know that they have an advocate
working to make the library of maximum value to them.

5. Programming

by

SANDY DOLNICK

with contributions by

Caroline A. Loose

Scott Bennett

Friends have programs to raise funds, to increase public awareness of library resources, to increase public and member recognition of the Friends organization, and to recruit new members. Programming reflects the Friends orientation to the membership and to the general public. Broad-based public library Friends might prepare exhibits and popular lectures, for example, while a university group might choose programs with a narrower, more academic appeal.

Except for perhaps the annual meeting, it is unlikely that any single Friends activity will attract the entire membership. And since all communities and library constituencies are different, there is no combination of programs or number of events that will succeed everywhere. To a considerable extent, each group learns by experience. Some events are successful beyond all expectations while others fail inexplicably. A variety of programming that is relevant to the needs and resources of the library, the interests of the Friends membership, and the characteristics of the surrounding community is best.

Friends in large cities have different problems from those in small towns. Large cities have more resources to draw upon but also more events in the community that compete for members' time. Libraries in smaller areas may serve as social centers; Friends programming should reflect this.

Figure 12 is a checklist in outline form for choosing one of the four major types of programs that Friends sponsor. Figure 13 summarizes the steps to be taken in planning the event once it has been selected. For the sake of simplicity,

the list assumes that the event will feature a guest speaker.
It can easily be adapted for other programs. Figure 14 is a
last-minute checklist. It lists all the details that must be
addressed to prevent physical discomforts to speaker and audience and to account for the income. Figure 15 provides a record
of the event and describes what can be learned from the planning experience.

PROGRAM CONTENT

Figure 12 lists the four general types of programs to consider before selecting one: social, educational, book-related,
and library oriented. Two major sources of program ideas are
the calendar and local newspapers. Seasonal activities are
always fun and can often be tied in with books; the Pomona
California Friends had a Laura Ingalls Wilder Gingerbread Social. Bus loads of Detroit Friends have attended baseball
games. Craft classes before the holiday season are often popular; people like to do these things in groups. The people
who sit and quilt might be the core of the group that makes
telephone calls or stuffs envelopes at another time. Often
the newspaper will announce events in town far enough in advance so that Friends can plan a program around them. If another organization is inviting a prominent person to speak,
for example, the Friends may arrange to have that person appear at their meeting, too. In many cases there is no cross-
over between the two audiences. The Friends can then share
costs with the other sponsoring organization.

Social Programs

Programs that are just fun, providing an excuse to get together for the library, are very popular. These can be free
or can have a large admission if intended as fundraisers. Examples of social programs include ice cream socials; "supper
in the stacks" with food brought into the library; dances
and theme parties (e.g., Roaring Twenties, Renaissance Fair);
dinner-theater evenings on chartered buses; tours of local
homes; open house for senior citizens; bus tours of a neigh-
boring city; and a midwinter tea for the library staff and
Friends. Academic groups have visited private presses, paper
makers, literary or historical landmarks, and even other libraries.

Educational Programs

These can increase awareness of special parts of the library's collection or can take advantage of community inter-

1. Purpose

    a. Raise funds
    b. Community good will
    c. Member recruitment
    d. Membership and public awareness of Friends
    e. Public awareness of library resources/needs
    f. Combinations of the above

2. Content

    a. Social
    b. Educational
    c. Book-related
    d. Library-related

3. Target audience

    a. Friends membership
    b. Membership and guests
    c. Community at large
    d. Community leaders by special invitation
    e. Special interest groups

4. Site

    a. Capacity sufficient for anticipated audience?
    b. Location
        (1) Accessible by public transportation?
        (2) Parking available?
    c. Possible sites
        (1) Library
        (2) Hotel or other public facility
        (3) Private club (clubs with a discriminatory policy
              should not be used)
        (4) Private home

5. Variables

    a. Time (day/evening)
    b. Food/beverage facilities; caterer
    c. Alcoholic beverages

Fig. 12.   Program planning checklist—Choosing the event

1. Before the event

    a.   Obtain speaker
        (1)   Correspondence with speaker or agent
        (2)   Payment
        (3)   Transportation (to town/hotel/meeting site)
        (4)   Welcoming arrangements
        (5)   Lodgings for speaker
    b.   Publicity
        (1)   Press release
        (2)   Arrangements for newspaper interview with speaker; possible radio/television appearance

2. Invitation
    a.   Date and time
    b.   Sponsor
    c.   Site
    d.   Admission price (member/nonmember)
    e.   Menu
        (1)   Food price (member/nonmember)
        (2)   Cash bar
    f.   Open to membership only/open to general public
    g.   Purpose
    h.   Program
    i.   Reservations
        (1)   Required/not required
        (2)   Reservation form (where to mail/phone number)
        (3)   Closing date (usually weekend before event)
    j.   Source of further information
    k.   Board member responsible for proofreading invitation

3. Involvement with other Friends committees

    a.   Membership
    b.   Publicity
    c.   Newsletter
    d.   Hospitality
    e.   Fundraising

Fig. 13.   Program planning checklist—Planning an event

Fig. 13.   (Cont'd)

4. Book and author sale of books

    a.   Person responsible for ordering
        (1)   Where orders are sent
        (2)   Number of books needed
    b.   Event arrangements
        (1)   Pricing (sales tax included?)
        (2)   Tables for display and sale
        (3)   Provision for making change
        (4)   Person responsible for collecting/counting money
        (5)   Security
    c.   Return of unsold books

5. Arrangements at event site

    a.   Equipment
        (1)   microphones
        (2)   speakers
        (3)   tape recording equipment
        (4)   blackboards
        (5)   easels
        (6)   podium
        (7)   projection equipment (screen?)
        (8)   lighting (spot/flood)
        (9)   decorations (check fire laws)
      (10)   flowers and plants
      (11)   flags, banners, and signs
    b.   Head table (seating; place cards)
    c.   Extra chairs, tables readily available?
    d.   Person designated to introduce speaker
    e.   Printed programs
    f.   Photographer

1. Before the event

    a.   Check facilities
        (1)   Meeting room, open and staffed?
        (2)   Seating style, as ordered?
        (3)   Cooling/heating operating?
        (4)   Sound system operating?
        (5)   Lectern in place; light operating?
        (6)   Ice water/glasses at speaker's table?
        (7)   Ashtrays in room?
        (8)   Projection equipment operating/projectionist on duty?
        (9)   Blackboards/easels/signs/banners/flags/lighting/ flowers and plants in place and as ordered?
      (10)   Photographer present?
      (11)   Groups' name listed at entrance?

2. Event

    a.   Registration/check-in
        (1)   Provisions for handling money
        (2)   Bulletin board for announcements
    b.   Presentation of gift to speaker

3. After the event

    a.   Count and deposit money
    b.   Pay bills for event
    c.   Thank-you letter to speaker

Fig. 14.   Program planning checklist—Last-minute details

1. Event or project title

2. Date

3. Location

4. Chairperson and committee members

5. Purpose of event or project

6. Basic information—describe briefly how the event was carried out.

   a. Pre-event
   b. Event
   c. Post-event
   d. Friends staffing
   e. Library staff involvement
   f. Library board approval (was it necessary, and when was it given?)
   g. Publicity
   h. Facilities and equipment needed

7. Proposed budget

8. Materials needed and cost

   a. Donated materials (with estimated cost circled)
   b. Total expenditures and income, noting profit or loss
   c. Source of materials (if unusual)
   d. Leftover materials and where they are stored

9. Problems*

10. Recommendations*

11. Additional comments

*Please check with your co-workers for problems and/or solutions they may wish to add.

Fig. 15. Report outline

ests. Many Friends, for example, provided information about
the Tutankhamen exhibition before it arrived in their area.
Educational programs can also be cosponsored with other area
groups whose interests are similar to those of the Friends.
Cultural organizations such as the local arts council, symphony, opera, or museum Friends, and ethnic cultural organizations may be willing to supply exhibits, speakers, or even
entertainment such as folk dancers, without charge. Government
agencies often have exhibit materials and speakers available
for workshops and lectures. Candidates for political office
and representatives of political interest groups are often delighted to have an opportunity to appear before an audience
of Friends. Examples of educational programming might include
concerts and art exhibitions of all kinds; presentations on
local history and genealogy; classes and workshops in crafts,
gardening, puppetry, or legal issues such as estate planning
and taxes; voter information; and cardiopulmonary resuscitation (CPR) training.

Library-Related Programs

Increasing public awareness of library resources and needs
is a basic function of Friends. Though National Library Week
in April is a natural time for such events, they should be
held year round. Programs might include demonstrations of how
to use the library or special library equipment and systems
(inter-library loan, data base searching); library tours;
showings of films or videotapes from the library collections;
and programs on such special aspects of library work as the
preservation of rare materials. Children's Book Week falls in
November, and is an obvious opportunity to gear an event to
children. Academic libraries often gear programs to the opening of special exhibits in the library. These are sometimes
showcases for new acquisitions, but could also be "faculty
choice" or the highlighting of a special collection.

Book-Related Programs

These are an obvious choice for Friends. Since they may intimidate some persons who do not read widely, public library
Friends should not rely upon them exclusively and should have
some book-related programs that are popular in nature. Appearances by local or nationally-known authors, illustrators, or
photographers often draw good audiences. Academic Friends have
programs on book collecting and other bibliographic subjects,
including private press printing. Book study or review groups
have proven popular, as have programs in which books are reviewed or discussed by the librarian, a local authority, or a

panel of experts. Some Friends have sponsored courses or discussion groups that focus on the Great Books, while others
have developed programming about books on such single topics
as cooking, art, travel, or children's literature. Writing
contests or workshops have been successful.

Book sales or book fairs are familiar events. They are the
most popular money-makers of academic Friends groups. Normally
there is an annual sale; some Friends have reported as many as
four sales each year. Book sales can range from simple fundraisers at which donated volumes and library discards are sold
at low prices to elaborate affairs of regional importance, featuring rare works at substantial prices and thousands of bargain volumes laid out on long tables under a tent. Such events
usually make money, provide much opportunity for volunteer activity, bring many people together, and generate good public
relations for the library.

SPECIAL TOPICS

Cosponsorships

It is vital to find ways to introduce new audiences to
Friends programming, thus expanding potential membership and
increasing visibility of the group. Because the library has
material that appeals to every interest, there is virtually no
limit to the types of groups that can be included in cosponsor-
ship of programs. Groups have held programs in conjunction with
the following organizations:

School District	Symphony Friends
Recreation District	Town Meeting
Women's Club	Garden Center
Altrusa	Arts Council
Arts Center	Museum Friends
PTO	County Extension Office
Book Club	Historical Society
Welcome Wagon	Conservation Commission
Repertory Theater	Internal Revenue Service
Medical Center Auxiliary	Civic Roundtable
Theater Friends	Senior Citizens
Kiwanis	Investment Brokers
Lions	Civil War Roundtable
Business and Professional	Gourmet Society
Women's Club	Film Society
International Relations	
Council	

Author Appearance

Should Friends wish to have an author speak, the organization can organize the event in several different ways.

1. Find out if local television stations, newspapers, or department stores know of any author who is coming into the area. Contact the publisher to learn if the Friends can be included on the tour.
2. If the Friends group has a particular author in mind, the publisher should be contacted. Names and addresses are listed in *Literary Market Place* and several other reference works. The Friends should tell the publisher which author is desired, the potential size of the audience, the type of event contemplated, whether the author's books will be sold, and whether money is available for an honorarium. Travel expenses should be discussed; all arrangements relating to the author's appearance should be made in writing. If the Friends' first choice is not available, the organization should tell the publisher whether a substitute is acceptable.
3. If the Friends group has no particular author in mind, it may choose a publisher and state the group's interests. If, for example, the organization wishes to have a program on history or gardening, it may select a firm that publishes many books in these fields. The publisher may have an author on tour already who would be willing to appear before the Friends.
4. Cosponsoring an author appearance with another organization can lower costs and increase the audience for the event. In some locations, the local newspaper will act as cosponsor. In other areas, several small Friends may combine for a joint meeting with an author as speaker.
5. Not every author makes a good speaker. If it is possible to communicate with a person or group which has heard a particular author in the past, a check of the speaker's ability can be made before committing.

Annual Meeting

Once each year the Friends must have a business meeting at which officers are elected and annual reports given. This occasion need not be dull. It can be combined with a reception, a speaker, or even the official opening of an exhibit.

Keeping Up

Since events must often be planned months in advance, the

Friends will try to predict future trends in the book world to some degree. *Publishers Weekly* and *Library Journal* are two periodicals that announce books well in advance of publication. They often tell if an author is planning a promotional tour. If a particular book seems likely to appeal to the membership, a program can be planned near the time of its publication. The library may be asked whether it plans to buy the book and the publisher may be asked to include the Friends on its tour.

Each group has to learn what type of programming is best for them. Once a program has proven successful, it should become a prototype for another program within the course of the next program year. In that way the Friends will build a reputation in the community for a particular effort. This enhances their image, but also allows for experimentation as less successful programs are replaced by further attempts at interesting the public in the Friends of the Library.

A continuing source of program ideas is available in the *Friends of the Library National Notebook,* which is published quarterly.

Experience mixed judiciously with experimentation is the basis for the correct programming formula for each group. This is one area where outside influences over which programmers have no control can make a disaster out of a potential success. Bad weather, local crises, and economic conditions all have to be taken into consideration up to a point, but since there is no one date that is perfect, just as there is no one program that is exciting to all, once the decision is made to go ahead, the best the program chairperson can do is plan carefully for all contingencies, and hope for the best.

6. Your Public Image

by

ANNE J. MATHEWS

SCOTT BENNETT

with contributions by

Gloria Glaser

In order to describe what Friends groups do in various types of libraries and how they work in communities, with boards of trustees, the library staff, and political groups, it is necessary to have brochures, letters, and press releases. Membership, programs, fundraising, book sales, lobbying, and services are all advertised and supported by brochures, flyers, invitations, letters, posters, and fact sheets. These efforts are an integral part of Friends groups.

Although there is no substitute for the personal enthusiasm of Friends for the library and of the librarians for the Friends, specific types of materials are used by Friends groups around the country to inform their communities about their activities and programs. Many of these examples illustrate the basic concepts of effective public relations.

"Public relations" has been defined in a variety of ways. At the most basic level, it could be described as "relations with the public," which include good manners, common sense, and effective communication; public relations means doing a good job and telling people about it. It involves library goals and policy, staff attitudes, and the communication of opinions and ideas to all members of the community which the library serves. A more formal definition is provided by J. Carroll Bateman, former president of the Public Relations Society of America: "Public Relations is the planned effort of a business organization or other institution to integrate itself into the society in which it exists." In today's rapidly changing world, it is essential that the changing goals and roles of libraries be articulated to the many publics they serve, as well as to those from whom they seek support.

Effective public relations always addresses the who, why, how, and what questions. This chapter attempts to apply these basic questions to public relations activities of Friends.

WHO

The *who* of this chapter are libraries of all types and sizes in all parts of the country: public libraries large and small, academic libraries, and special libraries. Friends organizations are often considered the public relations arm of the library. They know the community, are known in it, and can communicate effectively with the groups in the community from which they come. Most of all, they care about the library.

Academic Friends have the same goals as their public library counterparts, but operate under somewhat different conditions. For academic libraries, the geographical spread of potential Friends is normally much wider and the loyalty that prospective members feel may be to the college or university rather than to the library specifically. Indeed, the Friends may compete with other fundraising activities of the institution. It is often true as well that a widely dispersed Friends group does not have a direct and highly visible impact on an academic library. Friends can and often do play a key role in maintaining library excellence. But theirs is a supportive activity; however important it may be, special care must be taken to maintain its visibility.

In most instances, volunteers do public relations work for Friends. These are laypeople who wish to support their library and who take responsibility for planning programs and for informing their community about the Friends. Some Friends have members who work professionally in public relations or advertising; these people may volunteer their skills. Large libraries which have public information officers, graphic designers, and printing equipment may be able to help the Friends write and print their materials. Every Friends group should use its imagination in seeking public relations help.

For academic Friends, circumstances are again somewhat different. The first people who do public relations are often those who have a direct professional interest in the library— librarians and some faculty members. As the membership grows, this founding group will soon consider how best to involve such laypeople as alumni or persons from the surrounding community. It is important that these laypeople possess an understanding of the library and its needs so they can represent it effectively. It is important too that they have substantial responsibility for Friends activities. Their satisfaction with their own effectiveness in promoting good public relations for the library is a key to how willing lay members are to invest their energies in Friends work.

Responsibility for academic Friends public relations comes down to a question of whether the Friends are largely an independent, self-sustaining group of volunteers, with lay leadership drawn from, and responsive to, the general membership, or whether the Friends are directed by persons professionally interested in the library, who, in effect, must sell the library's activities and needs to the membership. Both approaches are workable and can be effective; elements of each model of operation can show up strongly in both. How much autonomy a Friends group will have bears upon its ability to manage the library's public relations effectively.

The target audience for Friends public relations varies according to the purpose of the publicity. Newsletters and annual reports usually go to all Friends, while announcements of book sales or public meetings are sent to newspapers and radio and television stations. Brochures, posters, membership materials, and program flyers may be mailed to all library card holders; to members of social, literary, athletic, and other organizations; to PTA groups; businesses; faculty and students; library staff members; churches; clubs; and city officials—in other words, to all those individuals and groups whom the library is prepared to serve.

WHY

Friends do public relations to support the library, to raise funds for it, to attract special gifts, and to improve public awareness and understanding of the library. The purpose of Friends has been described earlier; communicating that purpose is the reason for doing public relations.

For example: the library has large print books for people with visual problems. Friends volunteers are available to bring these books to people who cannot travel to the library. In order to get the books to the users, Friends may prepare public service announcements for the radio, make phone calls to social agencies who work with handicapped or elderly people, and send letters to nursing homes.

Other opportunities for public relations may include the opening of library exhibits, introduction of new services, lectures and other meetings, or important new library acquisitions.

When Friends groups embark on fundraising projects to support a unique collection for a library, or sponsor a series

of programs or assist in special services, they publicize
these events in a variety of ways. The format may vary, but
the purpose is consistent: to focus the attention of the public on the activities of the Friends group and the services,
the collection, the facilities, and the programs of the library. The library board establishes goals and makes policy.
The library staff implements these goals. Friends play an
important role in telling the community what the library
goals can mean to them.

Two or three significant programs a year, which are well
prepared and presented, or a series of "brown bag" lunch
talks which involve authors, community leaders, or legislators, make newsworthy stories. A cautionary note: *Before
planning and advertising anything, communicate with the library director in order to avoid duplication of effort*. Remember that Friends work on a team with trustees and library
staff.

HOW

How do Friends groups advertise? *How* do they communicate?
As has been suggested, all media are employed in public relations. Newspaper personnel may best be approached in person, depending on community practice. If you live in a large
circulation area you must determine which department—education, book, society, or metropolitan—will be your best contact. Call for an appointment and go in person to meet the
editor. Explain whom you represent, and ask if there are specific requirements for news announcements for this paper. If
you have a fact sheet or brochure explaining the purpose of
your Friends group, take it along. If you do not, use the
"purpose" statement in your charter or constitution, and
write a brief statement; just be sure to have something in
writing, which has your name, address, and phone number on
it and which you can leave with your contact.

Television, like radio, makes public service time available for nonprofit associations—the Federal Communications
Commission encourages this. You can use this time to promote
your group, your membership drive, your fundraising, or the
library. Your library may have spot announcements available,
and Friends can help by contacting local stations and taking
these "spots" to station directors, if the library wishes.
The American Library Association has excellent radio announcements, featuring well-known television, sports, and literary
figures. If your library does not own these, they are available for a modest cost from ALA Public Relations. Perhaps the
Friends could purchase them for the library! Hints on pre-

paring radio and television announcements as well as press releases are contained in the recently published *PREPARE! The Library Public Relations Recipe Book,* available from the Library Administration and Management Association of ALA for $4.00. Your local stations may also be willing to assist you in preparing this material. They have trained personnel and they are always alert to items of interest for the community. Frequently it is all a matter of "we have not because we ask not."

WHAT

After a review of hundreds of pieces of public relations literature issued by Friends across the country, one statement must be made. Do nothing unless you do it well. Public relations need not be lavish or costly but it must communicate. Someone in the Friends organization will have writing or graphics knowhow. Ask for help or solicit advice from the library staff, from the local college, or from a journalism or art teacher. Look at the materials of other community organizations, choose those that work well, and find out how they were done. There is always help around—look for it!

One other general comment may seem so basic that it should not need to be made. Put the Friends name, address, and state on all pieces. Many items which were submitted to the ALA "Swap 'n Shop" program (held annually during the ALA convention) or sent as samples to the ALA Friends Committee lacked the city or state where the library was located. Phone numbers with area code should also be placed on all items.

Publicity and Advertising

Friends may produce attractive publications at low cost by following these suggestions:

1. Copy that will be reproduced directly should be typed on a machine that produces clear, even impressions. An electric typewriter with a carbon ribbon is best. If the machine has interchangable type balls, headings and special information can be produced in large, attention-getting typeface.
2. Headlines and titles can be made with precut letters, dry transfer lettering kits, or special machinery. A good stationery, office supply, or art supply store will have items of this type.
3. Ready-made copyright-free art is available in books or sheets. It can be clipped out and attached to a page with rubber cement. Quite elaborate art, including alpha-

bets, frames, ornaments, borders, and numerous kinds of
illustrations, can be purchased in book form. The leading
source of such material is Dover Publications' Pictorial
Archive series.
4. Offset printing is slightly more expensive than the
   older mimeograph techniques but superior in appearance.
   A good printer can advise the Friends.

All of the following kinds of publicity and advertising were
submitted to the survey committee:

Stationery with letterhead. This was on white, buff, green,
or gray stock, mostly 8½" x 11½". Several pieces show sketches
or small photographs of the library while others have a logo.
Some samples also include the names of the Friends board or
library trustees. In all cases, the design is attractive and
fulfills its mission of presenting a positive public image of
the Friends group. Friends of the Philadelphia Free Library
had a design contest to create a Friends logo or symbol that
became common to all Friends literature. The winner was
awarded $25 and later put his design into sketches for letter-
head, notepaper, and press release sheets. He later entered
these items into the Philadelphia Art Director's Show.

Notepaper. This usually had a sketch of the library, 3½" x 4½",
when folded. Artist credit and "Sold by the Friends of the
_____ Library" is printed discreetly on the back. No
price is indicated, but this is heavy stock with the etching
done in sepia. A similar, but larger, single-fold piece of
notepaper was submitted by a university Friends group.

Postcards. With a color photograph of the library on the front
and a five-line description of the library on the message side,
these came from two libraries. Again, the Friends were cred-
ited: "This postcard is a project of the Friends of the _____
Public Library." A second type of postcard bears a sketch of
a famous "feminist, author, and editor," and briefly describes
this woman, the town, and the library. On the message side is
written "Sold for the benefit of the _____ Library," and
the name of the city and state.

Invitations. Card-sized invitations to special Friends-sponsored events range in style from the formal (engraved or em-
bossed on vellum-type stock with return-reply cards enclosed)
to the chatty and informal ("Please Come"). (See figure 16.)

Bookmarks. These are inexpensive and flexible. Some solicit
membership: "Be a Friend. It's a great way to put your inter-

THE PRESIDENT OF THE UNIVERSITY

AND

THE FRIENDS OF THE COLUMBIA LIBRARIES

REQUEST THE PLEASURE OF YOUR COMPANY

AT A DINNER

ANNOUNCING THE WINNERS OF

THE BANCROFT PRIZES

IN

AMERICAN HISTORY

AND

DIPLOMACY

THURSDAY, THE SIXTH OF APRIL

NINETEEN HUNDRED AND SEVENTY-EIGHT

THE ROTUNDA, LOW MEMORIAL LIBRARY

Reception at six-thirty
Dinner at seven-thirty
Black Tie
Parking on College Walk, Enter from Broadway

Kindly respond
on the enclosed card
by March twenty-eighth

Fig. 16.   Invitation to the Bancroft Prizes dinner by the
           Friends of the Columbia (University) Libraries

est in the library to work. Ask us." Others suggest action:
"Give us your used books." "Volunteers are needed now." These
two bookmarks were part of a coordinated publicity effort.
They carried an angel motif and the slogan, "Be an Angel. Be
a Friend."

Other forms. Friends may spread their publicity through small
ads in other publications, by means of a variety of printed
materials, and through events. Friends may place a brief message in the library's general brochure or may use a small
square in the library newspaper to solicit new members or to
announce the time and place of the next meeting. The group
might also make posters with news of its programs, fact sheets
about the library, sample letters to legislators in support of
library goals, and brief descriptions of Friends accomplishments. The Friends may choose to write to influential people,
such as the PTA president of every school in the city.

Different groups have produced decals, book plates, printed
paper, and plastic or cloth bags with a Friends message. The
cloth bags may be used to carry such library materials as
phonograph records or art prints. One Friends group inserted
each new library card in a folder which said, "Now that you
have a library card . . . be our Friend." When opened, this
card became a 4" x 5" brochure with a brief description of the
Friends and a membership form.

Friends which sponsor unusual programs have advertised them
in unique ways. Friends of the San Francisco Public Library
presents a "Talking Library." Speakers are available to groups
and organizations to make ten to forty-five minute presentations on such topics as San Francisco history, rare books, reference information, and funding of libraries. These speakers
and their topics are announced on an 8½" x 11" three-fold
mailer brochure which opens into a poster.

One program which is a major fundraiser and publicity-get-
ter is sponsored by the Littleton, Colorado, Friends. Called
"Fiasco," it is a musical spoof of people and events of the
city. Now in its tenth year, it involves forty to sixty people,
and during the four nights of its run, more than two thousand
came to see it. "Fiasco" raises funds and both generates and
receives much publicity. There are preliminary newspaper, radio, and television announcements, handsome programs and posters, and follow-up stories and pictures in the local newspaper.

Publications

Brochures. Perhaps the most popular form of public relations
is the brochure. These range from very sophisticated and

elaborate three- or four-fold items on expensive paper stock, with pictures and illustrations, to very simple, low-cost dittos.

In planning an informational brochure, or any other piece, determine the *audience* for which it is intended, the *message* to be conveyed, the *number* to be printed, and how frequently it must be updated. Make the message brief without sacrificing clarity or persuasiveness and tell the reader what to do, e.g., "Join the Friends," "Attend this program," "Come to the book sale," "Write to your councilman or legislator," or "Send a donation."

Different pieces with different approaches may be needed for various audiences. Do not hesitate to copy ideas from others! The *Friends of the Library National Notebook,* published quarterly by Friends of Libraries USA, has many excellent ideas. Most Friends groups are delighted to describe their experiences. The *1978 Directory of Friends of Libraries* lists other Friends who might supply information. Additional sources are listed in the bibliography.

Brochures are as diverse in format and content as the Friends who prepare them. They carry a variety of messages:

> *Why be a Friend?*—Statement of purpose
> *Library news and calendar of events*—History, rules, programs, services, hours, and a paragraph about the Friends
> *Membership brochure*—Itemizes the Friends accomplishments, annual events sponsored by the Friends, the time and place of monthly meetings, and incentives for joining. These always have a tear-off sheet or half sheet with an application form (see chapter 4).
> *Exhibit brochure*—Describes special collections of rare books, books by local authors, topical exhibits, and new art prints. Many of these general library brochures carry the imprint, "This brochure is a courtesy of Friends of the Library."
> *Special services*—Lists such services as the "Pony Express" (figure 17), through which Friends take books and other materials to shut-ins. These brochures are often left at nursing homes and hospitals.

In addition to the one- or two-fold brochure, special flyers are popular. Some are 8½" x 15" or larger and can be used as posters, while others are postcard size or 8½" x 11". All carry messages similar to those described above.

Monographs. These are quite common. Many measure 6" x 9" and have sixteen pages or more. Some are occasional publications

FRIENDS OF SOUTHBURY PUBLIC LIBRARY
Southbury, Connecticut 06488

PONY EXPRESS

The Pony Express is a book delivery service operated by the Friends of the Southbury Public Library.

Volunteers will pick up and deliver books from the Library to residents of all ages who are temporarily or permanently homebound and who live in any part of Southbury.

There is no charge for this courier service which offers books and magazines of all kinds, some of which are in large print.

For more information call:
The Southbury Library (264-6373), or
Mrs. Coverly Fischer
Chairman of Pony Express
(264-4397)

Fig. 17. Card describing the "Pony Express" service for the homebound of the Friends of Southbury Public Library

while others are part of a numbered series. Friends might
sponsor a monograph on their twenty-fifth anniversary. The
publication would contain a history of the library as well
as the Friends. Monographs can also describe the interests
and concerns of various library departments in a series of
essays. Special collections in academic, large public, and
special libraries are annotated in book and booklet form;
many are handsomely illustrated. The Sacramento City-County
Library Friends sponsored a writing contest and published
the winning entries in a ninety-four page anthology. Some
monograph publications are free to those Friends whose membership falls in the "patron" category, while others are
available for a modest price or a donation.

Newsletters. Friends newsletters range from single typewrit-
ten sheets printed in one color without a logo to two-color
typeset papers with a logo. Frequency of issue varies from
occasional to ten or twelve times a year. Friends news sometimes appears in the library newsletter. In some cases, the
library issues no publication and the Friends newsletter is
the only source of library news. Alternatively, the Friends
may supplement the library newsletter.

Newsletters are important. They tell members that the
Friends organization is interested in them. The newsletter
is a membership benefit for it provides news of Friends,
recognition, and a means of directing volunteer work.

Through the newsletter, Friends learn of future activities
and programs. Details can be provided that would not appear
on an invitation. The membership can be introduced to officers
and other important Friends. The newsletter also can provide
information about the library. At the very least, it reminds
Friends of the group's existence and needs.

Outstanding volunteers, donors, and new members can be
recognized in a Friends newsletter. Recognition is an important form of compensation to people who have donated services
or money. The newsletter may make less active members feel
that they are missing something. The newsletter can also describe how Friends help the library and what kinds of volunteer services or donated equipment is needed. If the Friends
newsletter is just circulated to the membership and given
away at the library circulation desk, it is missing its most
important audiences: the general public and such special interest groups as businesspeople, political leaders, senior
citizens, and minorities. Friends should seek wide distribution for the newsletter. A supply should be made available
to each group that uses the library meeting room. Copies
should be included in Welcome Wagon packets.

It is important that the Friends newsletter be clearly

written and a pleasure to the eye. Otherwise, the Friends
will fail to communicate with the membership and the general
public as well. If no Friend has professional writing and
graphics experience, the organization should seek advice from
some outsider such as a newspaper editor, a teacher of English
or journalism, or an artist.

Annual reports. Many Friends produce annual reports. These
range from a special issue of the newsletter to a separate
publication. Annual reports can supplement a newsletter. They
provide a sense of continuity to the group, an opportunity for
summarizing past accomplishments and announcing future plans,
and a place for public recognition of outstanding Friends and
donors. Annual reports can also project a positive image of
the library in order to increase citizen support. The report
should always contain a membership blank. The same rules suggested for newsletters apply to annual reports as well:

Know the target audience
Distribute widely
Keep information timely and pertinent
Encourage new membership
Make the publication simple, modest, and effective
Recognize contributions in time and money
Tie in with publications produced by the library.

A FINAL WORD

It has been stated and demonstrated here that effective
public relations always goes beyond publicity. The image of
the library, and of the Friends group, the personal relationships which library staff and volunteers have with others, the
development of cooperative community efforts, lobbying, and
fundraising are all part of the larger concept of public relations. It is often the image, rather than the printed or spo-
ken word, which makes the impact on those various publics to
whom the Friends organization is selling its program.

For further information, see the bibliography. One item of
special interest, mentioned earlier, is *PREPARE! The Library
Public Relations Recipe Book*. Pages 53-63 of this volume contain an excellent annotated list of books and articles relating to Friends and library public relations.

7.   Fundraising

by

JOAN ERWIN

with contributions by

Karen Lynne Furlow

Ann S. Gwyn

From meet-the-author luncheons to direct mail solicitation
to bass fishing tournaments, the possibilities for Friends
fundraising projects are unlimited. Many believe that the best
projects are those that relate to the general purposes of the
Friends. Others have fundraisers that do not relate in an obvious way to the library, but still help publicize the Friends
and the library they support.

Membership dues and donations are usually the first source
of income for Friends. Used book sales are often the first
real money-raising project. Beyond these, there is great variety in the kinds of fundraisers that Friends have. One Friends
group made a name for itself when it invited citizens to "Buy
a Brick" in the new library building. On some occasions, a
community-wide drive to raise money for a library listening
center, bookmobile, or even a new building has been the project that led to formation of a Friends group.

Many Friends organize meet-the-author events and charge admission. Others may receive a portion of the purchase price
of the author's books sold at such events. A cut of one-third
of the list price can add up to a good sum at a well-attended
event.

Friends can encourage private gifts to the library as memorials or honors for someone. Publishing a brochure that sug-
gests such bequests is one step toward making library users
aware of this possibility. (This chapter includes a case
study of a book endowment project.)

Academic or special library Friends, particularly those

that seek to raise substantial funds, may be compelled to make special provisions to avoid competing for donations with other special interest groups in the university community. Some academic Friends report a happy association with their alumni or university development office. These include Stanford, the universities of Colorado, Illinois, and Massachusetts, Cornell, Miami of Ohio, and Brown University. The alumni and development offices of these institutions are a primary source for the names of prospective Friends, who may already be donors to the university, and whom the library would never have thought to approach for funds. These universities solicit contributions from every graduate and identify the library or Friends as one of several campus units to which donations can be designated.

But since other groups on campus, such as Friends of the museum, the art gallery, or the music or theater departments may argue for equal treatment, the university may conclude that it will receive more unrestricted funds by limiting its cooperation with Friends organizations. In this case, the Friends may fare better as an independent organization.

A survey of Friends in health sciences libraries, conducted by the Houston Academy of Medicine, Texas Medical Center Library, reported that sixteen libraries had independent Friends and seven had Friends that were subordinate to a university organization. The independents contributed an average of $4,870 to their libraries each year. The subordinate groups provided relatively little money. Directors of the libraries whose Friends were subordinate to other groups reported the problem of competition with other university Friends both for funds and members.

If the Friends group contemplates an extensive fundraising campaign, it may consider employment of professional fundraisers. There are advantages and disadvantages to this. While such firms provide lists of prospective funding sources, tested organizational procedures, and professionally-produced brochures, they are expensive and still expect the Friends membership to make most solicitations. Local public relations firms that do some free public service work for the sake of good community relations may provide many of the same services. Hiring part-time office help can relieve the extra burden of paperwork in a large-scale fundraising campaign.

MEET THE AUTHOR

After book sales, treated in the following chapter, probably the most popular (and best library-related) kind of Friends project is the meet-the-author event. Local authors, the more recognized the better, are potential guest stars for coffees, luncheons, dinners, or talks to which admission can be charged. Even better crowd-builders are writers who must come some miles to appear before the group. Something about distance traveled enhances the appeal of a speaker.

Book/author dinners often feature two or three writer/ speakers on the theory that if one writer will draw some people, three can draw many more. Honoraria are not always necessary to get good speakers but legwork is. Sizable communities can try to obtain an author who is already on tour to promote a new book; publishers pay part or all of the expenses for such trips. Then it is up to the local group to lure a big audience to make the author's trip worthwhile. Sales of the new book (autographed by the author after the speech) and the publicity generated for the author and the book are benefits to both author and publisher.

The local newspaper or broadcasting station may cosponsor the event with the Friends. That helps assure good publicity and may bring in some money to help with the expenses of the event. Book stores and department stores with book departments are also potential cosponsors that might welcome the opportunity to promote their books.

Meet-the-author teas or wine and cheese parties or full-fledged dinners have been held in the library in some communities. One Friends group called its in-house fundraiser "Dinner in the Stacks," and offered a dance floor in the children's story room. Obviously some library buildings (and some library directors) are better than others for such events. There is obvious public relations value to having Friends events in the library to remind participants that the event is being held on behalf of that community institution. In-house projects also lure nonusers into the building for a glimpse of what the library might offer.

CASE HISTORY

The Friends of the Orlando Public Library established a Book Endowment Fund to provide a channel for sizable donations and to accommodate the desire of people to participate in the growth of the library.

The Friends invite donations of $150 to establish a book endowment that provides each year in perpetuity a worthwhile book in memory or in honor of a person (figure 18). (The $150 is invested and the interest earned buys a book each year.) A handsome endowment certificate, printed on parchment-like paper, is sent to the person honored or the family of the person memorialized, as designated by the donor(s). A bookplate

Friends of the Library Book Endowment, Inc.
Ten North Rosalind
Orlando, Florida 32801

I wish to participate in the establishment of a Book Endowment. Enclosed is my check for $ _____

made payable to Friends of the Library Book Endowment, Inc.

Income from each $150 Endowment is to be used to purchase annually a worthwhile book to be

placed in the _____ Library of the Orlando-Orange-Osceola Library System.

in memory of _____

in honor of _____

SEND NOTIFICATION OF ENDOWMENT TO: Date _____

Name _____   Signed _____

Address _____   Address _____

_____   _____

Orlando Public Library System
Ten North Rosalind
Orlando, Florida 32801

I wish to donate a book to the library in honor of _____

in memory of _____

Enclosed is my check for $_____ **made payable to the Orlando Public Library System.**

Please select a worthwhile book to be placed in the _____ Library of the

Orlando-Orange-Osceola Library System.

SEND NOTIFICATION OF DONATION TO: Date _____

Name _____   Signed _____

Address _____   Address _____

_____   _____

Fig. 18.   Flyer from Friends of the Library Book Endowment, Inc.,
Orlando, Florida

Fig. 18. (Cont'd)

establish a book endowment or donate a single volume

Here is your opportunity to give pleasure to others while helping to preserve the memory of a special person or honoring someone you admire.

Establish a Book Endowment or donate the cost of a single volume in the name of the person to any of the eleven libraries in the Orlando-Orange-Osceola Library System.

A book plate will be placed in each book giving the name of the person in whose honor or memory the book is given and the name of the donor or donors.

If you like, you may suggest some subjects for book choices that would be appropriate.

BOOKS AS TRIBUTES

Honor books can
● Salute a retiring club officer
● Mark a birthday or anniversary
● Thank a business or a friend for a special favor

BOOKS AS MEMORIALS

A book memorial is a fitting expression of sympathy and a lasting tribute that continues a person's influence in the community.

A BOOK ENDOWMENT

provides **each year in perpetuity** a worthwhile book for any unit of the Library System designated by the donor.

AN ENDOWMENT MAY BE ESTABLISHED:
● for the full amount of $150.
● in the form of negotiable securities.
● in three $50 installments
● by family groups, friends or organization members who have accumulated a total of $150.

An Endowment Certificate will be sent to the person honored or the family of the person memorialized as designated by the donor.

Each Donor will receive a receipt for his tax-deductible contributions.

A suitable public record will be kept of the Book Endowment.

A book plate will be placed in each book each year giving the name of the person in whose honor or memory the book is given and the name of the donor or donors.

TO DONATE A SINGLE VOLUME:

Give the Library your check and this information:
● the name of the person to be remembered, as it should appear on the book plate.
● your name as it should appear on the bookplate
● name and address of person to be notified
● your address (for the card of acknowledgement)
● subjects of books that would be appropriate (if you like)

An appropriate announcement will be sent to the person you wish to be informed of the gift. The amount is not mentioned.

Book donations are tax deductible.

a book is used.... and it lasts

is placed in each book each year giving the name of the person honored and the name of the donor.

The endowment can be established in the full amount of $150, in three $50 installments, or by family groups, friends, or organization members who have accumulated a total of $150. The donor receives a formal printed acknowledgment that also acts as a receipt for his tax-deductible contribution (figure 19).

Endowments are given to salute a retiring club officer, to mark a birthday or anniversary, or as an expression of sympathy. Perhaps half of them are established with checks from several people totaling $150. Usually a group of friends or family members combines to buy a book endowment. After six or seven years, $15,000 has been accumulated to purchase one hundred endowed books each year.

To start the endowment project, the Friends incorporated "the Friends of the Library Book Endowment, Inc." with the same officers as "the Friends of the Library of Orlando." They opened one savings account to receive the $150 donations; checks are made out to Friends of the Library Book Endowment. At the end of each year, FOL turns over to the library's book budget all of the interest that has accumulated that year. The principal ($150) from each donation remains permanently in the savings account (or another investment account earning more interest).

In many situations, a Friend volunteer (or a committee) mails acknowledgment of the donations and keeps records of donations and book selections. The Library's Community Relations Office does this in Orlando. The Friends treasurer deposits the donations and handles all contact with the bank.

Donors are invited to designate an interest area (figure 14) from which books should be chosen from each endowment each year; some endowments are directed toward travel or local history or antiques. Most are left open to the discretion of the person making the selection. As each endowment matures in its anniversary month, a library staff person chooses an attractive volume from the available new books on their way to the shelves. In other communities, a volunteer could handle this job.

It is rarely necessary to order a special book to fill an endowment. A beautiful book already chosen by the library receives the book plate, and the endowment is filled each year with worthwhile books that are needed in the collection. The endowment income pays for that book and boosts the book budget by that amount.

Usually the purchase price of the selected book is more than the $9 or $10 interest actually earned by the invested endowment. The library simply absorbs the difference in cost

A word of appreciation from

THE FRIENDS OF THE LIBRARY BOOK ENDOWMENT, inc.

We gratefully acknowledge your contribution toward an
HONOR BOOK ENDOWMENT

When completed it will provide a book each year in
perpetuity for the Orlando-Orange-Osceola
Public Library System.

An Endowment Certificate has been sent to the Honoree.

A word of appreciation from

THE FRIENDS OF THE LIBRARY BOOK ENDOWMENT, inc.

We gratefully acknowledge your contribution toward a
MEMORIAL BOOK ENDOWMENT

When completed it will provide a book each year in
perpetuity for the Orlando-Orange-Osceola
Public Library System.

An Endowment Certificate has been sent to
the Family of the Deceased.

Fig. 19.   Cards for book donations to the Orlando-Orange-Osceola
Public Library System

in its regular book budget. (It is possible that the library
discount price that comes from quantity buying is near the
amount of interest earned.) The public relations value of
having such attractive books for endowment selections is obvious; the bookkeeping actually necessary to charge the dis-
counted price against the endowment records would be time-
consuming and unproductive.

A file on each endowment records the name of the donor and
the person honored or memorialized; the names, addresses, and
contributions of the contributors; additional information such
as a subject area towards which the endowment is applied; and
a list of the titles and authors of the books purchased with
the endowment. In the first year or two of the project, Orlando
sent a notice of the book chosen to each donor. This practice
has been discontinued for several reasons: the cost in time
and postage, the difficulty of maintaining an updated address
for donors, and the irrelevance of such a gesture after a few
years.

A Friends Book Endowment project can be as simple or as com-
plex as the group wishes to make it. It can be handled entirely by volunteers or with the support of library staff. It is
one more good way to enable the community to show its support
and appreciation of the library.

Whatever method is used to raise funds, there is one iron-
clad rule: *Always recognize the donor*! Whether a person gives
one dollar or ten thousand, that sum represents a portion of
his or her income. Whether the donor is named on a brass
plaque, listed in a book on permanent display in the library,
recognized in the Friends annual report or newsletter, or just
thanked with a personal note from the president, something is
needed to make the donor aware of the importance of his or her
gift. Many organizations want that dollar and it is plain common sense to thank people for favors received.

PLANNING

All fundraising events or programs must be planned with
great care. The Friends should begin by setting a dollar goal
and by appraising its assets realistically. If the group has
only a few working members, it cannot expect to carry out a
complicated program. Friends with much free time and the willingness to donate it are assets. So are members with experience
in fundraising events. The Friends must estimate how much seed
money will be needed to set up the event and when these funds
must be available. It must also attempt to predict the potential audience or public participation in the event or program.
Winning the Money Game, published by Baker & Taylor, is a

collection of case studies of library-related programs and events that can serve to raise money.

However unlikely it seems, unusual events have also raised funds for libraries. House tours, theater parties, art auctions, bridge marathons, fishing tournaments, sailing regattas, walking or running marathons, and a rooster crowing contest have all raised money for library support.

As long as certain basic elements are part of a fundraising campaign, there is no limit to the types of ways to raise money. There must be a recognized use for the money, an estimate of how much is needed, a target group of donors, an opportunity for making donations, and recognition of receipt of the money. Much record keeping is involved. Fundraising is a difficult task, but one of the most vital that a Friends group can perform.

8. Book Sales

by

GLORIA M. COMINGORE

Book sales are the most popular form of fundraising and community involvement for Friends, regardless of the size of the library. Whether held at intervals during the year, or as annual or semiannual events, the sale of donated books and/or library discards can focus publicity on the Friends and the library as well as produce income

A great deal of organization, preparation, and volunteer help will make a successful book sale a reality.

COLLECTING

Sale books, records, and magazines are public donations or library discards. Donations are solicited all year long by various means; it is important to make it as easy as possible for the public to contribute. Book barrels should be placed in each library lobby. The barrels should be large and attention-getting. Colorful posters on each barrel might read "Friends of the Library—DONATIONS."

A great deal of attention should be given to publicity requesting contributions, as well as to publicity for the book sale itself. Books are solicited in several ways:

1. Printed or mimeographed notices asking for book and record donations should be placed at check-out desks of all branches of the library.
2. News releases asking for donations should be sent to local area newspapers and paid advertisements solic-

iting books should be placed in free community newspapers. (Note: In some areas the Friends jeopardize their
chances for public service time, if they use paid ads
elsewhere.)

3. Notices can often be included with the city's water bill
   mailings, or as stuffers in monthly statement mailings
   from banks and credit card companies. Contact city hall
   or local banks and other firms which have regular mailings.

4. Posters can be placed on bulletin boards at grocery
   stores, elementary schools, high schools, colleges, and
   many other places with much public traffic.

Arrangements must be made with volunteers or library staff
to transport donated books to the work area for the book sale.
The books should be collected all year long, and the book sale
chairpersons should have a well-organized procedure for handling the material as it is received so that the work does not
pile up and become overwhelming.

SORTING, PRICING, AND BOXING

Fortunate book sale volunteers have a convenient work area
with rows of book shelves. Each shelf should be marked with a
category, such as "fiction," "technical," and "how-to." The
categories into which the books are to be sorted should be decided by the chairpersons when work begins on a sale. The categories should be diversified enough to provide easy customer
selection and yet not so numerous that confusion results when
displaying books at the sale.

The chairpersons, or designated volunteers, should sort the
books as they are received and place them on the shelves.
Shelves can be labeled "not priced" and "priced." Experienced
volunteers can then price the books and place them on the
"priced" shelves for later boxing by Scout groups or volunteers who prefer to do this type of work. In a smaller operation the same volunteers may sort, price, and box books, and
these steps can be eliminated. But some willing and hard-
working volunteers dislike pricing or sorting, for example,
and can be very helpful in labeling and filling boxes.

The approach to pricing depends on the objective of the
sale. If the sale is to raise money, then the books should be
priced to maximize the income to the library. If the purpose
of the sale is to dispose of books culled from the library
collections, then the books should be priced low to get them
into the hands of those not able to afford them at regular
prices, overlooking the profit motive but providing good public relations for the library. Items that are too good to

throw away, but not good enough to sell, should be set aside during the year for a "free box" at the sale.

Volunteers sorting and pricing books should be alert for first editions, rare, old, or expensive books. These should be handled separately, priced by someone with knowledge of such books, and displayed on a "collectors' table" at the sale. Persons responsible for sorting these books should visit used book stores and read publications such as the *Antique Trader* to familiarize themselves with examples of rare books. Pricing guides in the library's reference section are valuable in determining sale prices for such books.

Pricing books is difficult because it is subjective, but volunteers should be as consistent as possible in their pricing throughout the year. Prices should be fairly reasonable, as one objective of a book sale is to make customers feel they got a bargain and want to come back the next year.

Volunteers who price books should visit book stores, other book sales, and garage sales to become familiar with selling prices of various types of books. Experience at each year's sale is helpful also. If books on politics do not sell well, for example, be sure they are priced low in the following year. It is helpful to have volunteers with expertise in certain categories, such as rare books, children's books, and records to price those items. Experience has proven that their evaluation is usually fair, accurate, and acceptable to the public.

Book sale chairs may consider having informal pricing meetings to go over the pricing policies for each category of books in order to provide fairly standardized prices at the sale. Pricers should take into consideration scarcity, condition, level of interest, number and quality of illustrations, and retail prices. Sets of encyclopedias should be judged according to age, quality, condition, and completeness. Magazines and *Reader's Digest* condensed books are usually plentiful and should be priced low.

Chairpersons should decide, before any pricing is done, exactly how the books are to be marked. Marking prices with ink is damaging but avoids the problem of prices being erased at the sale. Prices should be marked in the same place on each book, and in the same manner, to speed up check-out during the sale.

After the books have been priced, they should be placed by category in boxes with lids which can be folded shut for storage. The category of books in each box should be marked on all four sides *before* the box is filled, for ease in labeling. The volunteers should make certain that each book has a price when it is boxed, and each box should contain only one category of books.

Boxes should be counted by category and these figures en-

tered on record sheets placed in the work area. These records
need only show "category" and "number of boxes." This box
count will help the chairs plan for the number of volunteers
and the amount of time needed to move boxes to the sale location; the amount of table space needed to display books at the
sale; and the number of signs required for the tables.

After collected material has been sorted, priced, boxed,
and counted, the boxes should be stored in one section of the
work area. This procedure should be followed from the end of
one book sale until the next one begins, to keep the work from
building up into a tremendously large and exhausting job.

ORGANIZING THE SALE

In addition to collecting and preparing the material to be
sold, the chairpersons must also see that the publicity chairperson has publicized the sale. This can be done by the same
means by which donations were requested. Announcements should
also be sent to local radio and television stations. Notices
should go to local parent-teacher associations and senior citizens clubs, bibliophile groups in the community, teachers
organizations, and book stores. It goes without saying that
the Friends newsletter should promote the sale.

The chairpersons should make certain that the treasurer
prepares for the sale by obtaining a permit, if needed; providing state sales tax schedules, if applicable, for use by
adding machine operators; and a sales tax form to be submitted
after the sale. The treasurer should supply coin wrappers,
bank deposit slips, a rubber stamp for the face of checks and
a "for deposit only" stamp, and currency and coins for the
cashier. The treasurer should be prepared to pick up cash from
the chairpersons several times during the sale.

A chairperson or a designated volunteer must schedule workers to transport boxes to the sale location, work during the
sale, and clean up afterwards. Using the box count, chairpersons can estimate the amount of time needed for preparing the
room for the sale. Charts should be made showing work shifts
and the names of volunteers scheduled for each shift. Make
certain that volunteers' phone numbers are included on these
schedules. An overlap in shifts is recommended to allow for
a smooth transfer of responsibilities and the possibility of
late arrivals. Local Girl Scout and Boy Scout troops can be
very helpful during book sale preparation and are often required to do such work for badges.

Chairpersons must arrange for the room or hall where the
sale will be held, and plan for tables and bookends to display the books. They must provide signs showing categories

of books and other signs required for the sale. They will need adding machines, extension cords, extra rolls of adding machine tape, cash boxes, and boxes and bags for the customers' books. Name tags and coffee supplies should be furnished for volunteers, and miscellaneous supplies such as pencils and pens, scissors, scotch tape and masking tape, stapler, paper clips, 4" x 9" and 9" x 12" envelopes for counting and storing money should be on hand.

In order to have a smooth running book sale, the chairpersons should think it through carefully and try to anticipate what will be needed. Once the sale begins, the pace will be frantic.

Friends can be admitted to a special presale before the sale opens to the public. Memberships should be available at the door and many people will come early to join at that time. Chairpersons must make arrangements for a membership table to be set up and operated that evening to handle these new members as well as renewals.

During the sale it is advisable to have one or more adding machine operators totaling the customers' books, and one cashier to take the money. At extremely busy times, such as presale night, two cashiers—one to take cash and one to take checks, if there is a policy that checks will be accepted—will help speed up the check-out line. One of the chairpersons should remove extra cash from the cash box as soon as it builds up over a minimum amount needed by the cashier. This should be put in a secure place, and should be picked up during the day by the treasurer for deposit in the bank. The chairperson and treasurer should both count the cash as it changes hands. A record sheet should be made of each transaction, showing the exact amount of cash and checks transferred, and signed by the receiver, the treasurer. This will give the chairpersons a running total of sales.

Books should be added to the tables as excess stock and space are available. As the sale progresses, prices can be reduced at the discretion of the chairpersons.

In order to dispose of all books collected, the last day or hours of the sale can be half price. This can be publicized by large posters or signs during the latter part of the sale. A specified time should be set aside for this half price sale. After this is over, customers may be asked to pay for the books they want, the room can be cleared, and, after a short interval, customers can be readmitted for a one-dollar-a-box book sale. Each customer may have all the books he or she can carry in a box for one dollar. Ordinarily this promotion, which should last at least an hour, will clear out all leftover books, and is a tradition to which book sale lovers can look forward each year. If there are books remaining after this, they can be sorted and those of good quality can be donated to nursing homes or veterans homes.

Checklists, setting forth their important duties, should be prepared for the book sale and publicity chairpersons and for the treasurer.

LIBRARY INVOLVEMENT

In an ideal relationship, library staff members work very closely with the Friends in development of the book sale and other programs throughout the year. Their help is valuable in all phases of preparation for the book sale and during the sale itself. The library's professionals can give valuable advice and assistance with pricing. Discards from the library are an important part of the inventory of a book sale, and volunteers should work closely with staff members in processing these books. Library helpers are usually needed to help with the heavy work connected with a sale, and the library's facilities may be needed to help produce and distribute flyers, posters, and signs. During the sale, the cooperation of the library's staff is vital, as volunteers will need assistance in a variety of ways. The presence and support of staff members at the book sale and other programs serves as a great source of encouragement to the Friends, and the camaraderie enjoyed is an important bonus.

Proceeds from the book sale can benefit the library greatly. The Friends may have been working towards a goal previously established with information provided by the library director, or may use the money in any number of ways. If a gift is purchased, it should be marked "Gift of the Friends of the Library," to mark the many hours of volunteer time that make up a successful book sale.

9. Lobbying and Legislation

by

SARAH C. HITE

Almost every library in the country depends upon federal, state, or local government for a substantial portion of its budget. These funds are allocated by legislative bodies which Friends can—and should—attempt to influence. There is probably no area more important in which Friends, either individually or as an organization, can make an impact. On a long-range basis, the Friends most significant achievement may well be the securing of adequate budget funds or convincing the public that bonds or a tax increase are needed for a new library building or for other essential capital improvements. As one Friend who was involved in legislative activities said, "Why should I slave over a book sale to make a few thousand dollars when I can talk to the city councilmen and get *many* thousands more for our library."

Because they are citizens who have chosen to volunteer on behalf of the library, Friends are often its most effective advocates. It is expected that professional librarians will speak on behalf of their libraries. They have a job to protect, after all. In many cities, the librarian is hired by city officials and is accountable to them. It may therefore be difficult for the librarian to speak out as he or she wishes. Library trustees also have a vested interest in the library. They may be political appointees who are not free to criticize city officials. Such problems do not affect Friends. The very existence of a Friends organization is proof that the community needs a library and that citizens are willing to support it.

Most elected representatives are conscientious people who wish to do their work and to be reelected as well. They are approachable and they do respond to their constituents. All elected representatives need help. They cannot make informed decisions without knowing the facts that Friends can provide. They always want to know what the voters are thinking. They must be told that citizens believe strongly in the importance of libraries, that library programs are really needed, and that budget cuts will affect the community.

The Friends must carefully consider how much time and money they spend on lobbying. This is necessary because of the way in which federal guidelines for tax-exempt organizations are written. These are described at the end of this chapter.

LOBBYING PROGRAMS

The primary purpose of Friends lobbying is *money*—either increased funding or maintenance of a status quo budget. All government budgets today are under intense pressure. The Friends must emphasize the importance of library funding to legislative decision-makers.

If the primary purpose, or a major purpose, of the Friends organization is to create good will for the library, half of the battle is won. If the library maintains high visibility in the community, maintaining the budget or increasing it should be easier. Through good publicity, Friends can ensure that the community knows of the services and programs that the library provides. Elected officials in the community should receive the Friends newsletter and literature that the library publishes. A Friend can be assigned to send photocopies or original clippings of library news and feature stories directly to local and state officials on a regular basis.

All lobbying activities by Friends *must be* coordinated with the city librarian and the trustees. The Friends must present a united front with the trustees and the librarian.

One good way to coordinate legislative efforts is to form a legislative committee of the Friends. This committee can study the best way to make an impact; can research and study the issues; can draw up a timetable for action; and can be responsible for legislative activities.

Local Level

Lobbying begins with local officials. Know who they are. Invite them to the library for a special occasion. (Perhaps this could be tied in with National Library Week.) Give the officials a tour of the library. Many council members may

never have been in the library, may not have been there recently, and may have no idea of the great variety of services
performed. Keep them informed. The Friends may prefer to host
a dinner, luncheon, or breakfast meeting at the library instead of an open house. In any event, make certain that local
officials are familiar with the library.

The Denver Friends assigned a member to each of the council
members who lived in his or her district. The Friend then invited that council member to a special tour conducted by the
librarian. Denver then invited the council member to lunch
with the librarian. The legislative official was thoroughly
informed on library matters.

Election time provides an excellent opportunity to learn
and publicize the views of candidates on libraries. A Friends
organization cannot endorse a particular candidate without
risking loss of its tax-exempt status, but it can publish the
stands of all candidates regarding libraries. An individual
Friend working on a candidate's campaign can be an asset when
it comes to library matters. The Friends might sponsor a "Meet
Your Candidate" night in the library, at which time each candidate's stand on libraries is requested.

Fortunately, libraries in most instances are like mother-
hood and apple pie. Not many politicians are willing to be
against them. But with all the other demands for money,
elected officials must be reminded constantly that the library
has needs. The greatest foe of libraries is probably apathy.
Politicians need to be told again and again that most libraries serve a higher percentage of the public and affect it more
directly than any other government service. Friends should be
ready with statistics on the percentage of the population with
library cards, the number of books checked out each year, and
the frequency of library usage.

A politician might be interested in the results of a 1978
Gallup Poll on current habits and attitudes of library use
which said that about 51 percent of Americans aged 18 and over
have visited the public library in the last year. The "heavy"
library user (that is someone who has used the library over
25 times in the last year) is typically:

18-34 years of age
college educated
living in a household with children under 18
a resident of the eastern part of the United States.

The Friends may provide each elected official with a library
card. If the organization knows of the interests or needs of a
particular official, perhaps it can inform that person when a
book of interest arrives at the library. Providing such person-

al service may cause the official to conclude that the library
is important to the community.

Including politicians in Friends activities is another way
to gain support. Invite them to the Friends annual meeting or
some other event that will have a large attendance. Try to
choose a program that will interest the target individual and
try to have a Friend who knows the politician make the invitation well in advance on a personal basis.

Library budgets are drawn up by the librarian and trustees.
Friends should be familiar with the budget. They should know,
for example, how much money is being requested to support existing programs, which programs deserve further funding, and
which have outlived their usefulness. Since Friends cannot
help unless they are informed, the Friends newsletter should
include articles about the budget and the schedule for its
preparation and presentation to city officials. If the Friends
plan to lobby for the library budget, they must establish
their own timetable. Although informing officials should be a
year-long process, there are certain times when activity will
peak. While the budget in under consideration, Friends can
urge members to tell council members how important the library
is to them. Those Friends who plan to testify should prepare
carefully. Others should be encouraged to write letters. A
brief letter to an official describing the importance of the
library can be very effective. The more letters sent, the
greater the impact.

If it appears a library budget is in trouble, mount a coordinated campaign. This would include telephone calls, letters,
newspaper articles, and letters to the editor. Friends can
circulate a petition requesting adequate library funding. If
the situation is serious, the organization can publish a flyer
that tells what budget cuts would mean to the patron. Unlike
librarians and trustees, Friends can distribute these to all
patrons. When the budget is to be presented or discussed by
city officials, Friends should attend the hearing. One Friend
can speak on behalf of the "people," to say how important the
library is to the community.

The Friends should always thank supportive officials, let-
ting them know how grateful the Friends are. This can be done
in imaginative ways. The Friends of Macomb Public Library
threw a Cookie Crunch for their city officials when an increased library appropriation was passed. Impressive resolutions of appreciation were presented to attending officials.

Though lobbying for libraries is important, the Friend who
lobbies for libraries must keep in mind the entire scope of a
politician's activities. Don't be so entirely consumed with
library matters that you lose sight of the men and women representing you and their philosophy of government; try to con-

sider their needs and yours within the context of a legislative year (figure 20). The first consideration must be: "Is
the official doing a good job? Does he or she make decisions
deliberately after considering all points of view?" Politicians resent rude, myopic, one issue factions. They must always be treated politely and thanked for their time.

It is also important to be willing to compromise in order
to make progress toward an objective. If the legislative body
cannot provide all the requested funding but does increase
the budget, the compromise should be graciously accepted and
lobbying efforts increased for the next year.

State Level

Involvement at the state level requires considerable knowledge and preparation. It is absolutely essential to work with
the librarian, the state library association, and the legislative network for libraries in the state. Friends can participate fruitfully in the state library association's legislative
committee.

Friends should acquaint themselves with the budgeting process at the state level so they know what roles the governor
and the state legislature play. As work on the state budget
proceeds, the Friends should contact the governor, the governor's advisory staff, and state budget analysts. Depending
upon circumstances, personal visits, letters, or phone calls
may be required.

Each Friend who is involved in state level lobbying should
learn how the legislative process works: the introduction of
bills; the legislative committee structure; and consideration
of bills on the floor of the legislature. Such information
can be obtained from a state legislator, from the League of
Women Voters, or from any public library.

Friends should know the names of the state representatives
from their districts. They should know what appropriations
are being requested at the state level for libraries and how
much of these monies will come to their library. The librarian
should keep the Friends organization apprised of the bills,
legislation, and proposed funding. In cooperation with the librarian, a campaign can be organized to tell legislators the
importance of library funding and what it will mean to constituents. A Friend who knows a legislator personally can be helpful in explaining the significance of library funding and any
new proposed legislation that affects libraries. If the Friend
does not feel adequately knowledgeable, it may be possible for
the Friend to arrange a meeting with the legislator and the
librarian.

A Friends-sponsored dinner meeting can provide a time for

Schedule of key events on a yearly basis:

STATE LEGISLATURE

January or February: Department of Education budget hearing before the Joint Budget Committee (JBC). This includes the Denver Public Library as the Colorado Resource Center (CRC) receiving state funds administered through the Colorado State Library for non-resident reference service.

January - March: Contacts are made with legislators, especially those on the JBC to solicit their support for the CRC.

April: The Long Bill is presented to each house for approval. At this stage if the JBC's recommendation in the Long Bill falls short of 100% funding for the CRC, legislators of the majority party in each house are contacted for their support of amendments for increased funding to the CRC. This happens in the party caucus before approval of the Long Bill in each house.

May or June: The Long Bill is adopted.

Summer and Fall: The Friends and staff contact and meet with legislators to make them aware of the Denver Public Library and how it functions as a State Resource. The concept of reference service is stressed at this time so the legislators have a comprehensive understanding of how reference service makes the Library a more effective resource to its users. (In election years Representatives and many Senators cannot be contacted until after the November election.)

Fig. 20.   Legislative committee information sheet—Friends of the Denver Public Library

Fig. 20.   (Cont'd)

CITY COUNCIL

Ongoing: The Staff of the Denver Public Library has
                    a newly formed "Personal Librarian Program"
                    which established a service whereby a de-
                    signated library staff member provides in-
                    formation on a personal basis to selected
                    city officials including city-councilmen.

Ongoing: Friends contact their city councilmen and
                    councilmen-at-large emphasizing the impor-
                    tance of the Library to the Denver Commu-
                    nity and the necessity of maintaining the
                    library's budget at a status quo level or
                    increased level.

March: Friends give input to the Denver Public
                    Library Commission regarding their sugges-
                    tions for the Library's following fiscal
                    year's budget.

March - April: Public hearings are held by the Commission
                    to solicit input from citizens for the
                    following fiscal year's budget.

June: The Commission submits requested budgets
                    to the Mayor's office.

June - September: Contacts with Mayor and City Council that
                    have been occuring on a regular basis are
                    intensified to keep the Library in the
                    forefront before the Budget Hearings.

September: Hearing of Library Budget before Mayor and
                    City Council. A member of the Friends makes
                    a brief statement in support of the Library
                    at this hearing

October: Budget is finalized.

legislators to be informed in some depth, to ask questions, and to exchange opinions with library personnel in a leisurely, relaxed atmosphere. If legislators and their spouses are invited, a high percentage of attendance is usually attained. The Friends president might contact the legislators by telephone, indicating the nature of the meeting, possible dates, and other attendees. Two or three dates should be suggested and the informal nature of the evening should be stressed. Written invitations should then be sent to the legislators with the selected date and time. All trustees, library directors, city managers or mayor, and council members should also be invited. If the topic is controversial, the press should be made welcome. Using place cards, the seating should be arranged so that legislators are distributed evenly. The Friends group pays for the dinners of the legislators and spouses. The presentation may include information on why libraries are important to the people of that area, the role of programs supported by the level of government represented by the legislators, and the status and problems of financial support from that level. The legislators should receive written summaries of the presentation and a written description of library services. An exhibit could show the types and varieties of library materials, especially those supported by appropriations of the legislators. Slides showing local facilities and people using libraries might be appropriate. Thank you letters should be sent after the meeting. Arrangements can be made to make the presentation privately to any legislator unable to attend the meeting.

In Denver, all state legislators representing the city were invited to attend one of several luncheons at the library sponsored by the Friends at which time the city librarian gave a presentation of the needs for state funding and how Denver libraries would benefit.

As in the case at the city or county level, it is important to know the calendar of events. Timing is important. Work should be done throughout the year, not only at the time of crisis. At the beginning of a legislative session write letters or make phone calls; personal contact is helpful because that tells elected officials what issues are of importance to their constituents. Members of a particular committee should be contacted or written when library legislation is pending before that committee. Another important time to write or make contact is when a bill is about to come before the full legislature.

Friends should learn when bills affecting libraries are going to be discussed in committee or on the floor. They should go and listen to these sessions to show the legislators they are interested. Hearings on bills or proposals are open to any citizen and a Friend should attend the important ones. Minutes of hearings and copies of bills are all available to the public.

Once a year many states have a Legislative Day, at which time librarians, trustees, and Friends converge on the capitol to inform legislators on library matters. West Virginia in particular has an outstanding event organized by the state library. Many Friends are involved with Florida's Legislative Day. The fact that concerned citizens are involved in addition to professional librarians makes an impact.

National Level

Much legislation that affects libraries is passed at the national level. Financing for library grants, building construction, and revenue sharing all come from Congress. These revenues can be very significant at the local level. Two recent examples of important legislation for libraries are the Copyright Law and the enabling legislation and funding for the White House Conference on Library and Information Services.

It is again important that Friends be informed. The librarian can provide information on pending bills that pertain to libraries. Most libraries have Congressional directories and basic government documents. The American Library Association is an excellent source of information. Congressional and senatorial offices will provide general or specific information. They can send information on current Congressional activity, proposed bills, existing laws, related regulations, and on current programs and available funding. Providing information to citizens is a routine function of these offices.

With the requisite information in hand, Friends should write or contact their representatives in Congress. Friends should say how the pending legislation will affect the library and the community. Because few citizens take the time to write when their direct financial interests are not involved, a letter from a Friend who has no vested interest will have great impact.

Though Friends can write at any time concerning a bill, there are times when a letter will have maximum impact. The most important is the subcommittee stage, before a bill is submitted in its final version. If your senator or representative is not a subcommittee member, write the subcommittee chairperson or chief counsel directly, sending a copy to your senator or representative. Once the bill is on the floor, write legislators again expressing your views and ask them to explain the position they will take.

When funding is involved, there are authorization and appropriation bills. Authorization bills allow spending up to a certain limit. Getting these funds through appropriation bills, coming from the Appropriations Committee, is often difficult. Write again. These bills actually determine how much will be available for the coming fiscal year.

Below are some simple rules for letter writing.

Address the legislator properly (figure 21).

A typed letter is preferable, although legible longhand is acceptable.

Be brief and to the point. Do not write a report. A post-card addressing the issue with the reason for support or disagreement is fine. Do mention the fact that he or she is *your* senator, representative, etc., if that's the case. This is very important.

Discuss only one issue at a time. Refer to the bill by num-ber or cut an article out of the paper and enclose it. Then the recipient knows the issue immediately. Explain your *personal* involvement with the issue or the local viewpoint. Tell how the proposal would affect your li-brary and community.

Support your arguments: "Because it is right or good" is not enough! Use your own words, stationery or letterhead.

Be courteous. Thank the legislator for giving attention to the matter, or just a plain "Thank You" letter for some-thing he or she has done that met with your approval.

Keep a copy of the letter for your file. When sending the same letter to more than one legislator, the courteous thing is to send originals to each. If you are sending a letter to a government official not in your district, copy it for your own legislator.

Request an answer. Ask the legislator how he or she stands.

Above all, don't hesitate to write. It's a few minutes work. America is one of the few places that you even have the option.

BONDS FOR LIBRARIES

In the event that city or county officials, the librarian, and the trustees determine that the library needs to be re-placed, extensively renovated, expanded, or supplemented by an additional building or a branch, Friends can be of para-mount importance in passing the necessary bond issue.

Before officials actually make the bond proposal, Friends can participate with the explicit cooperation of the board and librarians. Friends might be involved in the planning study that is undertaken to identify the need and to amass the data necessary to support the proposal. Friends can sug-gest that such a study be undertaken, can assist in gathering

How to Address

Councilmember: Councilmember_____

Mayor: The Honorable Mayor_____

State Representative: The Honorable_____
Representative from District_____
The State House of Representatives
State Capitol Building
City, State

Dear Representative_____
Sincerely,

State Senator: The Honorable_____
Senator from District_____
The State Senate
State Capitol Building
City, State

Dear Senator_____
Sincerely,

Governor: The Honorable_____
The Governor of_____
State Capitol Building
City, State

Dear Governor_____
Very sincerely yours,

U.S. Representative: The Honorable_____
U.S. House of Representatives
Washington, D.C. 20515

Dear Mr._____
Sincerely yours,

U.S. Senator: The Honorable_____
United States Senate
Washington, D.C. 20510

Dear Senator_____
Sincerely yours,

Fig. 21.   Letter writing—Forms of address

Fig. 21.   (Cont'd)

Vice-President: The Vice President of the United States
                      United States Senate
                      Washington, D.C. 20500

                      Dear Mr. Vice President:
                      Sincerely yours,

President: The President
                      The White House
                      Washington, D.C. 20500

                      Dear Mr. President:
                      Very respectfully yours,

---

facts, or can finance an independent study and publicize the
results.

Although Friends do not help in site selection, building
planning, and matters of that nature, they should be kept informed of progress. Once the decision for a bond issue or
property tax increase has been made, Friends can be of great
assistance in enlisting community support. They can call attention to the upcoming election and the benefits for the community if the bond issue passes. Friends may be able to contribute toward the cost of the campaign and may supply volunteer labor.

Friends have assisted with library bond issues by working
with other organizations, by registering voters, and by using
various techniques to publicize the issue.

Work with Other Organizations

It is very important to have a coalition of organizations
who support the issue. Meet with the chamber of commerce to
see how business might help. Write a letter to the president
of all leading clubs and organizations in the community,
urging their support. Ask for their endorsement. If this is
given, publicize it. Inform these people that the Friends has
a speaker's bureau and offer them a speaker for their next
program. Just before the election, write to religious leaders,
asking that they announce the upcoming election to their con-
gregation.

Voter Registration

Have a booth regarding the proposed bond issue at shopping

centers or grocery stores. Urge citizens to register and tell them how.

Publicity

Prepare and distribute an informative handout with facts and figures on the proposal. Distribute this at grocery stores and shopping centers. Mail it with utility, telephone, retail store, or bank statements. Send it home with school children. Have a supply available in libraries.

Print bookmarks with information about the bond issue. These can be sent home with school children and can be placed in libraries, book stores, etc. Bumper stickers can also be printed.

The Friends can establish and publicize a speaker's bureau and can sponsor sessions at the library outlining its needs, the purpose of the bond issue, and facts about the library. Neighborhood coffees can also be held.

Work with Media

The Friends should approach newspaper, radio, and television editors, telling them of the importance of the bond issue and enlisting their support. The librarian or a trustee should be included in these meetings. The Friends might also write a series of news releases focusing on different aspects of the library and the need for expansion. Individual Friends can write letters to the editor focusing on the reasons for the bond issue. It may be possible to have radio and television talk show hosts schedule an interview with a good speaker, the librarian, or a trustee. The Friends should also prepare public service announcements and distribute these to radio and television stations.

Immediately preceding the election, the Friends should have a paid ad in the newspaper. This could include the names of individuals, companies, and organizations that endorse the bond issue. Those who have lent their names to support the bond issue may be willing to contribute toward the cost of the ad.

Other possible publicity ideas include a float, bookmobile, or banner in any scheduled parade, posters, a large sign at the proposed site of the new library, a display model of the new library, a slide or movie presentation, and Friends in the bookmobile and in a booth at the library or shopping center to discuss the importance of the issue.

Immediately before the election, Friends should send out postcards to every registered voter. They should call regis-

tered voters urging their vote and should arrange necessary
transportation to the polls.

THE FRIENDS—TAX EXEMPT STATUS

There are federal guidelines that must be followed if lobbying consumes more than 10 percent of Friends *organizational*
time or money. Lobbying is defined as "carrying on propaganda,"
or otherwise attempting to influence legislation. The exposi-
tion which follows pertains only to Friends organizations *as
a whole* which lobby and the federal regulations that apply.

From 1934 until the Tax Reform Act of 1976, the Internal
Revenue Code provided that in order to qualify for exemption
as an educational or charitable organization (Section 501 (c)
(3)), "no substantial part" of an organization's activities
could be devoted to "propaganda, or otherwise attempting to
influence legislation." The phrase "no substantial part" was
never clarified, but it was generally believed that an organization could probably spend up to 10 percent of its time and
funds for lobbying purposes without endangering its tax exemption.

The Tax Reform Act of 1976 clarified permissible legislative activity. Now a tax-exempt organization (which all
Friends organizations should be) can remain under the "substantial part of activities" test or elect to be considered
in light of a "sliding scale" test. If the Friends decides to
stay with the "substantial part of activities" test, both *time*
and *money* spent must be considered. If it chooses the "sliding
scale" test, only money spent is considered.

Under the "sliding scale" test, a Friends group must determine each year the total amount of expenditures it has paid or
incurred for the charitable purposes for which it receives its
tax-exempt status. This includes administrative expenses and
expenditures for purposes of influencing legislation, but ex-
cludes all fundraising expenses. This net total is called the
"exempt purposes expenditure."

A tax-exempt organization may now spend 20 percent of the
first $500,000 of its tax-exempt purpose expenditure for pur-
poses of influencing legislation. If the exempt purpose expenditure is more than $500,000, this percentage decreases for
each additional $500,000. Within these limits, a separate lim-
itation is placed on so-called "grass roots lobbying," that
is, attempts to influence the general public on legislative
matters. Expenditures for grass roots lobbying may not exceed
one-fourth of the general limitation described above. Also,
any out-of-pocket expenditure which an individual (such as a
member of the Friends) incurs in lobbying on behalf of the

Friends must be included in determining the Friends' lobbying expenditures, even if the individual is not reimbursed for the expenditure.

If an organization exceeds its permissible limits (either the general limit or the grass roots limit), it will be taxed 25 percent of the amount by which it has exceeded the allowed amount. If a group exceeds its limits by an average of 150 percent over a four-year period, it will lose its tax-exempt status.

The 1976 Tax Reform Act also clarifies what is considered "influencing legislation." "Legislation" includes action with respect to acts, bills, resolutions, or similar items by the Congress, any state legislature, any local council or similar governing body, or by the public in a referendum, initiative, constitutional amendment, or similar procedure. The word "action" is "limited to the introduction, amendment, enactment, defeat of Acts, bill, resolutions or similar items." There are two general kinds of lobbying; i.e., "grass-roots lobbying" and "direct lobbying." As mentioned above, "grass-roots lobbying" is an attempt to influence any legislation by trying to influence the opinion of the general public or any segment of the public. "Direct lobbying" is any attempt to influence legislation through communication with any member or employee of a legislative body, or with any other government official or employee who may participate in the formulation of the legislation.

If, for example, one article in the Friends newsletter urges members to contact their officials, this would be considered lobbying. Only a pro rata share of the cost of the mailing would constitute a lobbying expenditure. If the newspaper or circular urging legislative action is distributed primarily to members, it would constitute direct lobbying. However, if more than 15 percent of the copies are distributed to nonmembers, the distribution of the newsletter or circular to nonmembers would be considered grass-roots lobbying.

The Tax Reform Act of 1976 also identifies certain activities which do not constitute "influencing legislation." These are:

1. Making available the results of nonpartisan analysis, study, or research
2. Providing technical advice or assistance to a governmental body or committee in response to a written request
3. Appearances before or communication with a legislative body concerning decisions which might affect the existence of the organization, its powers and duties, its tax-exempt status, or the deductions or contributions to the organization

4. Communication between the organization and its bona fide members with respect to legislation, unless those communications directly encourage members to influence legislation or directly encourage members to urge nonmembers to influence legislation. (Thus, if the Friends newsletter simply describes proposed legislation, informs members but does not ask them to take action, this is not considered lobbying.)
5. Communication with a government official or employee other than that which attempts to influence legislation.

As mentioned earlier, any organization with tax-exempt status under Section 501 (c) (3) of the Internal Revenue Code as an educational, charitable, or religious organization can elect to operate under the 1976 revised lobbying expenditure guidelines. (Exceptions are church-related organizations and private foundations.) An election (i.e., choice) by the Friends to have its legislative activities measured by the new expenditures test is effective for all taxable years of the organization beginning with the year in which the election is made. The election is made by filing form 5768 and stays in effect unless the Friends revoke it for a future year. It cannot be revoked while the year is in progress.

If a Friends organization is involved in many exempt activities, chances are that lobbying activities for the Friends as a whole would not constitute a "substantial part" of its efforts. If these efforts in time and money are less than 10 percent of the total spent, it may not be necessary to elect to be covered by the new rules. If, however, a great deal of time or money is spent in lobbying efforts by the Friends organization, the Friends might elect to come under the new guidelines.

There may be occasions in which a financial effort of such magnitude is contemplated that the Friends would lose their tax exemption or be subject to a substantial tax under the new elective provision discussed above. This might occur, for example, if the organization were to engage in a major campaign to support a library bond issue. Under these circumstances it may be desirable to form a separate organization to carry out this activity. Members could then be solicited and funds raised for this purpose. Contributions would not be tax deductible, but the funds could be spent on lobbying and legislative activities.

10. Portraits of Friends Organizations

by

PAUL T. SCUPHOLM

MARVIN H. STONE

ANDREA L. HYNES

SIEGFRIED FELLER

KENNETH A. LOHF

This chapter contains biographies of five Friends organizations. Paul T. Scupholm, Executive Secretary, describes the Friends of the Detroit Public Library. Marvin Stone, Fine Collections Librarian, tells the history of the Dallas Public Library Friends. Andrea Hynes describes the courageous efforts of a dedicated group of Friends committed to the support of their small local library. Kenneth A. Lohf, Librarian for Rare Books and Manuscripts at Columbia University and Secretary-Treasurer of the Friends of the Columbia libraries, contributes a lively account of academic Friends and the group at Columbia. The chapter closes with a brief history and summary of activities of the University of Massachusetts Friends of the Library.

FRIENDS OF THE DETROIT PUBLIC LIBRARY

The Friends of the Detroit Public Library, Inc., is a non-profit organization supported by three thousand individual members and more than one hundred corporations.

History

The Friends was incorporated in 1942 by leading citizens of Detroit to provide financial assistance to one of the nation's largest libraries. Today the Detroit Friends is a model of service and efficiency for the thousands of Friends organizations throughout the country. Detroit is first in the nation in terms of annual fundraising and second in total membership.

The Detroit Friends was the first to employ a full-time executive secretary, to pay its entire office payroll, and to assume the responsibility of recruiting and training volunteers to assist in various library departments and conduct guided tours. The Friends has provided several key collections with continuous financial assistance. Among these are: the Rare Book Collection, the Burton Historical Collection, the Business and Finance Department, the Technology and Science Department, and the National Automotive History Collection.

Membership has doubled over the past three years. The Friends credits this gain in support to its diverse areas of interest, unusual programming for members and general public, and to its plans for the future.

Leadership

The organization is governed by a volunteer board of directors which meets ten times a year. The board is comprised of men and women from the business, professional, and voluntary community. The financial affairs of the Friends are managed by a finance committee consisting of the major officers and the executive secretary, who is a full-time staff member.

Accomplishments

These leaders—the board of directors and the staff—have been responsible for many innovative windfalls shared by other libraries throughout the state. They secured tax credit status for Friends members from the State Treasury Department so that 50 percent of their membership donation becomes a tax credit. They have provided the services of their staff to other Friends throughout the country who seek advice and information. They have organized lectures, seminars, workshops, and numerous events that have attracted a wide spectrum of the Detroit area community. Sixty percent of the members live outside the city of Detroit.

The Friends public relations has given the library a favorable image in the community. Thus, in 1963 the main library built a new wing, doubling its square foot area, with contributions from the business community and individuals. Gifts to the Friends furnished the new Rare Book Room and a 375-seat modern auditorium. Friends Corporation members furnished several of the collections.

The Friends recently celebrated the donation of the one-millionth dollar to the Detroit Public Library. Several on-going projects are undertaken by subcommittees: the annual

Rare Book Auction sponsored by the Rare Book Council, a classic film and lecture series sponsored by the Detroit Film Society, and promotion and publicizing of the library's automotive archive by the National Automotive History Collection Board of Trustees. Each of these subcommittees of the Friends is involved in fundraising efforts.

Future Plans

The current major effort of the Friends involves creation of an endowment for the National Automotive History Collection. This archive needs new quarters, additional staff, and acquisition funds. The Friends has written a legal agreement with the Detroit Library Commission, establishing a twenty-five member board of trustees to oversee the creation and administration of the endowment. The trustees have autonomy in their decisions affecting the affairs of the collection with the understanding that they are an extension of the Friends board of directors. The trustees channel all funds through the Friends. Thus, the investments and legacies donated to the National Automotive History Collection are subject to the Friends experienced finance committee.

A recent Rare Book Auction netted $13,000 profit and has been made an annual event. Their Classic Film Series is now in its sixth season. Recent speakers have included directors Otto Preminger and Vincente Minnelli. Dinner/lectures continue to highlight the Friends programming activities. During 1978, Mary Welch Hemingway, Dr. John Gardner, and Archibald MacLeish spoke to full-house audiences.

The Friends plan to continue such activities in the future and look forward to new endeavors as they strive to enrich and maintain the reputation of the Detroit Public Library and its collections.

FRIENDS OF THE DALLAS PUBLIC LIBRARY

Founding

In 1950, community leaders felt an urgent need to correct the inadequacies of Dallas libraries resulting from the depression of the thirties, neglect during World War II, postwar inflation, and years of low municipal budgets. The library system consisted of a fifty-year-old crowded central library and five branches dating from 1914 to 1938. The bookstock was small and shabby, and the staff underpaid.

The Friends of the Dallas Public Library was founded at a meeting of interested citizens held on March 13, 1950. The

goal of the new organization was to "aid the Library by cre-
ating an awareness in the citizens of Dallas of the specific
needs of the Library and its functions."

The Friends donated a bookmobile to the library late in
1950 as its first project. Momentum carried into 1951 as funds
were raised to survey the library system, thus furnishing
guidelines for library rejuvenation.

New Central Library

In 1951 the Friends broadened its base of citizen support
by increasing membership to one thousand and turned to the
greater task of securing a new central library. The organization persuaded the city council to include funds for the
building on the May 2, 1952, bond referendum with the promise
that Friends would actively support the election in the community.

Support it they did, at a time when participation of non-
profit organizations in bond elections was permitted and encouraged. A speakers bureau arranged public forums and radio
and television interviews. A telephone committee called every
person holding a library card. The central library easily won
voter approval but soon encountered controversy over location.
The library board recommended the site of the original Carnegie building. The Friends supported this decision and, after
some time, it prevailed, permitting construction to begin.

Improved Collections

It was soon apparent that the new building would open with
shelves empty of books. In 1954, the Friends commissioned a
survey of the book collection and recommended a program of
enrichment. The central library opened in September, 1955,
with a newly organized young adult department stocked with
materials provided by the Friends. Friends also bought adult
books for the library and initiated a rare book collection
containing gifts from private libraries including a Shakes-
peare *Fourth Folio* and a thirty-five volume Diderot *Encyclo-
pedia*.

The Friends equipped the rare book room with cabinets,
furniture, and art objects. In 1961, the organization established the rare book collection as a special project with
$1,000 per year allocated for acquisitions. Individually and
collectively, Friends donated hundreds of volumes over the
years, including the *Nuremberg Chronicle*, a leaf from the
Gutenberg Bible, and illuminated manuscript books.

Other innovative materials collections instituted by the
Friends and later incorporated into the library budget were

the children's circulating picture collection (1964) and the environmental planning collection (1968).

Branch Libraries

With a modern central library a reality in 1955, the Dallas Public Library still lacked a branch system to serve expanding neighborhoods. The Friends sponsored a survey to study branch library needs and formulate a plan of expansion. The report recommended that Dallas retain four of its five branches and add ten additional units by 1970.

In subsequent years, the Friends helped the library staff and the library board to secure this branch system. The organization assisted in bond elections through personal contacts and funding to inform the public of library needs. Individual Friends occasionally assisted in site selection. The group also initiated a tradition of giving each new branch $500 for use as branch staff desired. Between 1963 and 1977, a total of fifteen branches used this money for audiovisual equipment, terrestrial globes, framed prints for home use, costly art books, and an oral history project. By 1978, the library had seventeen branches with two more on the drawing board.

Broadening Library Usage

The Friends also encouraged user activities within these structures. Mexican-American fiestas were underwritten in four or more branches each September beginning in 1968. These cultural and entertainment programs introduced library services to a large ethnic community. Black History Week provided a similar focus for exhibits highlighting accomplishments of black Americans. The "Showmobile" and the "Learning Scene" received support from the Friends in an attempt to bring library materials to low-income children who did not utilize branches. These brightly painted vans were provided with audiovisual equipment and puppet stages as well as traditional printed materials.

Strengthening the Library Staff

Ever mindful of the importance of expert staff to a service organization, the Friends eased a shortage of librarians in two ways. The organization funded a slide recruitment presentation showing the advantages of living in Dallas and working for the Dallas Public Library. Friends then underwrote part of the costs in 1963, 1965, and 1968 when library administrators visited accredited library schools to present this program to students. A number of librarians joined the library as a result of the visits.

The other approach to the personnel shortage was to improve qualifications of staff already employed by the library. A scholarship for summer study toward the master's degree was awarded in 1951 and repeated at irregular intervals until 1969, when an annual $1,500 scholarship was introduced. The amount increased to $2,500 per year in 1974. By that time the personnel situation had reversed itself. There was a surplus of trained librarians, but those already in service needed continuing education to stay abreast of advances in the field. The Friends accordingly designated these annual funds as grants to permit staff to attend workshops, conferences, and book fairs, and to bring experts to Dallas to instruct the staff. Many staff members benefited from scholarships and continuing education grants over the years. One employee assisted by the Friends received a doctorate and several completed the master's program.

Exhibits Program

Perhaps more national recognition has been forthcoming from exhibits than from any other activity of the Friends. Interest in the exhibits program began in 1955 with the opening of the new central library. The top floor of the building features a terrace room with glass walls overlooking a roof garden. The Friends endowed this room with equipment not included in the library budget. Carpeting, a track light system, draperies, a reception desk, and other extras were added year by year. The roof garden was landscaped in 1959 and 1965 and provided throughout the year with flowers. The terrace room and garden have served the library well as an exhibition-reception area.

Acquisition of display equipment figured in the Friends program. Two custom-made book display cases were donated in 1962 and a set of versatile free-standing panels with removable lucite showcases was purchased in 1975. Through the generosity of two longtime Friends, four specially designed rare book exhibit cases with ventilation and timed lights were added in 1977.

The Friends also provided annual funds for supplies and exhibit rentals. This amounted to $400 in the early years and increased to $1,200. Thus the library was able to offer outstanding year-round cultural and educational displays, some opening with preview receptions hosted by the Friends. The first major book show opened late in 1963. In all of the exhibits, Friends assisted with the planning, hosted receptions, served as tour guides, arranged for school tours, secured publicity, and paid for printed catalogs.

State and National Activities

The Friends of the Dallas Public Library established a cooperative link with the Texas Institute of Letters in 1960 by
donating through the institute an annual prize of $500 for the
best Texas book which makes a significant contribution to
knowledge. This is one of several book prizes which the institute awards to encourage writing in Texas.

The Dallas Friends organized in 1950 as an affiliate of the
state group, the Friends of Texas Libraries. This close relationship has endured. Two presidents of the Dallas organization also served as presidents of the Friends of Texas Libraries. The Dallas Friends has consistently supported the American Library Association and the Texas Library Association.

Public Relations

As a result of these accomplishments, the Friends has a
favorable image in the community. Communication has been encouraged as a means of accomplishing goals as well as gaining
new Friends. The public is invited to the annual membership
meetings which feature nationally known speakers. Each spring
since 1961 the Friends organization has invited several hundred civic leaders to luncheon at the library during National
Library Week. These "get acquainted" luncheons have no speeches
or agendas but instead encourage personal contacts and say
"thank you" to the leadership of Dallas.

The Friends and the Municipal Library Advisory Board have
maintained good relations, with the former careful to respect
the board's authority. The library board traditionally desig-
nates one of its members as representative to the Friends. The
same cooperative spirit has characterized relations between
the Friends and the library administration. The objective has
always been to help without impeding library operations. A
warm relationship has developed with the library staff which
fully appreciates the accomplishments of the Friends.

A bimonthly Friends *Newsletter* began publication in 1967 as
a means of informing members of activities. It is also sent to
libraries and library schools throughout the country to promote an exchange of program ideas.

While looking to the future, the Friends organization has
not neglected the past. It published a staff-written progress
report, "Five Years Forward, The Dallas Public Library 1955-
1960," as well as the comprehensive history, *Dallas Public Library: The First 75 Years* (1977). For the Dallas Public Library's seventy-fifth anniversary, the Friends in 1976 funded
birthday celebrations at the central library and all branches.

In 1975, the Friends had quietly observed its twenty-fifth

anniversary by donating a fifteenth-century Italian illuminated manuscript book, *Office of The Virgin,* consisting of
181 vellum leaves.

The Texas Library Association held its annual conference
in Dallas that same year of 1975. On that occasion, the association bestowed its Philanthropic Award on the Dallas Friends,
the only time this award has been given to an organization.
The award citation read, in part:

> The Friends of the Dallas Public Library was organized
> in 1950 when the Dallas Public Library had the reputation
> of being "the worst public library in the country." The
> objective of the original group of twelve founders was to
> "aid the Library by creating an awareness in the citizens
> of Dallas of the specific needs of the Library and its
> functions." On its twenty-fifth anniversary, 1975, the
> Friends of the Dallas Public Library still retains the
> same objective. Most importantly the group can point to
> countless accomplishments and, most significantly, work-
> ing relations between staff, board members, and municipal
> government have been positive and constructive.

The Future

Dallas voters approved bonds on June 10, 1978, for construction of a new central research library five times larger than
the existing building. The Friends helped inform the public
of the need for the facility. Private donors, mainly Friends,
pledged $10 million toward the $40 million construction costs.
The endeavor gave Friends the feeling that it had passed this
way before, except that in 1978, thanks in large part to its
own efforts, the city possessed central library resources and
a branch system which stood light years ahead of the 1950s.
Surely no city or public library can look to the future with
greater optimism—or closer Friends.

FRIENDS OF THE BONNEY LAKE PUBLIC LIBRARY

The Friends of the Bonney Lake Library provide a good example of what a small but dedicated group of Friends can do
to support their library.

Bonney Lake, Washington, became a city in 1949 with a population of 327. The population increased slowly until the 1970s,
when the city increased in size by more than 60 percent in a
seven-year period. In 1974 the city had no facility for library service and had not contracted for service from the ru-
ral library district. The local library board, appointed by
the mayor in 1972, had approached the state library and the

library district in an effort to obtain library service within
the city limits. However, the new city government had embarked
on a financial recovery plan at the same time. Library service,
although much desired, seemed beyond the city's resources.

In 1974 the members of the library board met with the library director of the district. They discussed the possibility
of a $150,000 grant for a new library facility. The grant
would involve a cooperative effort of the city, the library
district, and the local citizens.

While the details of the grant were formulated, the local
library board members began the formation of a Friends group.
The first mention of a Friends group appeared in an article
submitted by the board to the local paper. Board members spent
much of their time phoning and talking to citizens about the
grant and the need for library supporters. Three months before
the grant was awarded, a planning committee of ten citizens
including three library board members and a librarian from the
library district held a meeting. The group appointed a temporary chairperson and a temporary secretary. A general meeting
was planned for the following month. The committee used posters, flyers, and newspaper releases to invite interested supporters to participate.

The Washington State Library Commission approved the grant
for "a demonstration of system-oriented public library service
by Pierce County Library to the City of Bonney Lake for a
three-year period." By that time the Friends had elected five
officers, adopted bylaws, and filed for nonprofit status. Annual dues of five dollars were set and the Friends had twenty-
four members.

The Friends began an active existence answering a variety
of needs. The library opened for service in July 1975 and the
official dedication was held in September. The Friends helped
the library board by supporting the dedication program and
welcoming guest speaker, Dixy Lee Ray. Dr. Ray had returned
to the Northwest from Washington, D.C., and had not declared
her gubernatorial candidacy.

A second and immediate need met by the Friends was landscaping the library site. No funds were available to handle
this project and the Friends came to the library's aid.
Friends designed the landscaping and paid for the plantings.
In addition, Friends held work parties where everyone planted,
watered, and weeded the yard.

When the landscaping was under control, the Friends recognized the need for fundraisers. The following year they collected used books and records and held a two-day book, plant,
and craft sale. The funds raised were used to purchase garden equipment and a new bike rack.

During the summer the officers changed. The president and

the treasurer resigned and membership dwindled. The Friends
saw the need to formalize their approach to meetings and business. They resolved to conduct most meetings as board or working meetings for the planning of programs and activities. The
remaining meetings would offer programs to attract a larger
group of people and increase membership.

In the fall the Friends assembled to assist with the open
house that marked the library's first anniversary. Landscaping
activities continued. In January new officers were elected at
the annual meeting. The Friends then planned an ambitious
schedule of monthly programs.

Film shows and programs on energy conservation, library
materials selection, and home gardening were featured. The
year's most unusual and successful program was a benefit
staged in the local tavern. A noted local "pool hustler"
played his challengers with a household broom rather than a
pool cue. At the same time the membership committee launched
a mailing of membership brochures to five thousand city residents.

Once again, the officers changed in mid-year. The president
moved out of town and the membership chairperson position was
vacated. The attendance at work parties and board meetings
declined. The combination of continual hard work, high dues,
ambitious programs, personality differences, and changing officers discouraged membership. At the end of the second year
the real business of the Friends was carried on by a group of
four dedicated members.

New officers were elected in January and they began offer-
ing programs on a monthly basis. Crime Prevention, Meet Your
Mayor Night, Basic Steps in Genealogy, and a film/talk program about nature filming from Disney studios attracted a
growing audience and new members. Programs halted during the
summer and the Friends struggled in the fall to regain their
momentum. To increase membership the dues were lowered and
the membership brochure updated. At the end of their third
year most of the officers of the Friends were willing to continue holding office for another year. Thus, the current officers have had the benefit of learning from history. They
turned the landscaping function back to the library board.
They now hold monthly meetings throughout the year on an
established date. The Friends have promoted their accomplishments through newspaper articles and at every program they
offer.

Two years later it was decided to limit programs to only
a few a year, planned well in advance. During the past year
the Friends sponsored four special projects. Junior Friends'
Month, a series of four programs for teens, was held in the
spring. The Saturday morning series included a babysitters'

workshop, magic show, and back-packing and job hunting programs. At the Friends' invitation, Washington's governor returned to the library in July to celebrate the library's fourth anniversary. The Friends presented her with a lifetime membership in their organization.

In the fall the library board called upon the Friends to organize citizen support for a library bond on the November ballot. The Friends' efforts (telephone campaigns, newspaper ad, brochures, etc.) drew a large voter response. Although the majority voted in favor of the bond, it did not receive the required percentage for passage. Despite the final outcome the results were impressive for a first bond attempt undertaken on short notice. And the Friends anticipate organizing another support effort in the future.

As the final project of the year the Friends sponsored a family holiday program. The chorus from the local elementary school performed at the library and Santa Claus paid a visit. The packed library demonstrated continued community support and the need for a larger library building. To this end the Friends have planned a combination of both fundraising and program projects for their next year, which will continue to build community support for the library.

FRIENDS OF THE COLUMBIA UNIVERSITY LIBRARIES
History of Academic Friends

The association of academic libraries and Friends has been a long and venerable one, dating from the time of Sir Thomas Bodley, a distinguished diplomat under Queen Elizabeth I, who spent the last fifteen years of his life forming a library, not for himself, but for Oxford University. He inspired others from his group of "Honourable Friends" (a title the Bodleian Library uses today for its benefactors) to donate their books to the library as well, thus forming the concept of library benefaction. When he died in 1613, this charitable notion was to remain dormant for nearly three hundred years.

The first official group of Friends was that of the Bibliothèque Nationale in Paris, "La Société des Amis de la Bibliothèque Nationale," founded in 1913. This signaled the beginning of an era for academic libraries during which support was to become broad-based and contributions were to be made by quantities of individuals rather than only by a single benefactor. In 1925, the Friends of the Bodleian Library was officially established, and at approximately the same time the Friends of the Harvard Library was founded, largely through the efforts of Archibald Coolidge, at that time professor of history and director of the Harvard Library.

Columbia Friends

In 1926 in New York, Professor David Eugene Smith, who had retired from his Columbia University teaching position, founded the Friends group at Columbia, among the first such associations at an academic institution to be organized in America. The initial ingredients that went into the making of a successful Friends organization were great teachers who were lovers of books and generous alumni who did not forget the inspiration of their professors. Professor Smith, a much-loved teacher, who was also a prodigious collector of rare mathematical books, manuscripts, and instruments, was to become a major benefactor of his library. Shortly after failing health forced him to give up his Friends activity, the association died, testimony to the fact that the success of such an organization often depends on one individual's energy and enthusiasm. His activities did, however, establish a pattern of support for academic libraries in the decades to follow—to influence the donation of books and to secure funds for the enrichment of the collections.

The Columbia Friends was born again in 1951, and the mission of the group, as stated in its constitution and bylaws, was and remains:

> to promote and further among the alumni and the public an interest in the Libraries of the Columbia Corporation, to provide ways to give them a fuller understanding of the role of the research library in education, to serve as a medium for encouraging gifts and bequests in support of the Columbia University Libraries, and generally to assist Columbia University in showing through exhibits, programs, publications and by other means the resources of the University and its Libraries.

The aim of each Friends association will vary according to the situation at the individual library, but the above statement underscores the basic premises under which most such groups operate. Most importantly, implied in the above purposes are the promotion of an understanding of the library among a wider group of individuals than librarians and scholars themselves, and fostering of a favorable climate for support of the library over a broad range of possibilities. The governance and the program of each group, however, will vary according to local situation and need. For instance, a Friends group at a small college may find frequent meetings at the library of the greatest usefulness, whereas, at a large university in an urban area, an ambitious publishing program might be the best means of communication among members.

Administration

There is a degree of contradiction in the operation of academic Friends groups. On the one hand, a broader interest among outsiders can usually be attracted if the library and the Friends group are independent of each other, thus giving more freedom for support and for suggesting new means of benefaction. At the same time, the library and Friends group should cooperate closely, so that outside support remains in agreement with the goals of the library and its parent academic institution. These dual objectives can be satisfied through the structure and management of the association. A member of the professional library staff might assist in an active way in the operation of the group, and the head librarian could provide liaison with the library and its objectives without intruding directly into the functioning of the group. At Columbia, the university librarian is an ex officio member of the Friends Council, and the librarian for Rare Books and Manuscripts also serves ex officio on the council and as secretary-treasurer of the organization, an office to which he is appointed by the university librarian.

The government of the group is normally entrusted to a council or board, the members of which are usually appointed by the trustees of the college or university upon nomination of the president of the university. Nominations to the council are made in such terms of office as will result in continuity of operation. At Columbia there are eighteen council members, six in each of the three classes. The officers of the association, elected by the council from among its membership, consist of a chairperson, vice-chair, secretary, and treasurer. There are, in addition, standing committees, drawn from the council and the general membership, responsible for the various activities of the organization, covering such areas of interest as publications, programs, awards, memberships, nominations, acquisitions, and memorial books.

Membership

The members of academic Friends organizations come from a variety of sources, depending on particular places, individuals, and purposes. Persons on or near the campus, such as faculty, university officials, and librarians, may form the primary group. Persons among the alumni who have shown specific interest in book collecting and libraries will form an important segment of any academic group, but caution may have to be exercised in this area so that there is no conflict with alumni groups. In large metropolitan areas, the group may seek support from among the professions and the community

at large; these membership efforts will doubtless be modified
by the activities of other competing Friends in the area. Depending upon the goal of a specific group, membership might be
unlimited and support sought from the widest possible source,
while in a library with a more specific program, membership
might be limited to those individuals who, it is believed,
could best assist the institution in reaching such goals.
Broad support among great numbers is not necessarily the best
means to an end. A focused support among dedicated individuals
might accomplish the achievable goals more effectively and
efficiently.

Funds

Operating funds derive primarily from dues, and each organization will devise a schedule of classes of membership, i.e.,
regular, sustaining, patron, benefactor, etc., with each class
having a corresponding level of contribution. In addition, a
special membership for the institution's active and retired
staff members might be considered to encourage their participation. An honorary membership for those individuals who have
made distinguished contributions of their time or resources
might be devised. Dues contributions also provide funds for
the support of such projects as the acquisitions of important
first editions and manuscripts, endowments of library positions or book funds, purchase of equipment, furnishing a room,
to mention only a few of the projects which have been achieved
by successful groups.

Activities

Interest in a particular library and its resources can best
be stimulated through a series of meetings and receptions,
ranging from an annual dinner meeting with a featured speaker
to a reception opening an exhibition centering around an important library acquisition or commemorating a literary or historical anniversary. Libraries and Friends may sponsor annual
awards, such as the Frederic Bancroft Prizes in American History and Diplomacy at Columbia and the Donald F. Hyde Awards
for Distinction in Book Collecting at Princeton.

The publications of the Friends are an important means of
communicating to the members at large the projects and activities of the organization. The frequency of publication is important to maintain contact with the far-flung membership. For
example, the *Columbia Library Columns*, published since 1951,
is issued three times a year, in the fall, winter, and spring.
These publication dates generally conform to the meetings of
the Friends, and serve to record these activities as well. The

magazine primarily contains articles of general interest related to the library's collections. Each issue includes an account of individual gifts received during the preceding period. Entitled "Our Growing Collections," the account serves as a printed record of benefactions and indicates to the members of the organization how the resources of the library are developing, thus stimulating additional gifts. Other publications might include a newsletter, a bibliographical journal, keepsakes based on important books or manuscripts in the collection, and exhibition catalogs.

The number of Friends groups at academic libraries has increased substantially during the past thirty years. There is hardly an institution of any standing which does not now have a thriving organization stimulating interest in the particular library's development of research resources among faculty, alumni, and individuals. While such groups may at times assist in fundraising efforts, it is primarily the book and manuscript collections in the humanities, the arts, law, medicine, and other specialized areas which are their chief interests. Time and changing needs of libraries may place greater emphasis on the fundraising potential of Friends, but it would appear that the most successful among them achieve these goals as well if they are successful in their literary pursuits.

FRIENDS OF THE UNIVERSITY OF MASSACHUSETTS LIBRARY

History

The Friends of the Library began with the establishment of a board of temporary faculty trustees, which was succeeded by a new group of trustees, formally installed at the first annual meeting, November 15, 1970. The constitution calls the purpose of the organization "enrichment of the total resources and facilities of the University of Massachusetts Library."

Funds

A modest income is derived from annual membership contributions from individuals. Associate alumni campaigns have been very helpful in recruiting alumni for the Friends. Most of these individual contributions come from alumni and/or faculty, but some donations are received from students and other citizens. In 1971, the Friends received a grant of $25,000 from the Charles Merrill Trust. Other contributors have included university student and alumni organizations, foundations, and corporations.

Another regular source of income during the past few years

has been the annual Friends book sale. Books, magazines, and recordings are contributed for this purpose and, if not needed for the library collections, are offered for sale, usually in early October. The gross has been near $2,000 in each of the last three years, with proceeds used to buy books for the library.

Activities

Books purchased with Friends of the Library funds are identified with the name of the donor, unless otherwise requested. When a subject preference is expressed, the donor's wishes are honored. If no preference is expressed, the Friends selection policy guidelines are followed, with emphasis on Massachusetts local history and culture and a few other special interests.

Of the $42,000 expended from the Friends of the Library trust fund during the past six years, 95 percent has gone for books and microfilms. The remaining $1,930 has been spent for such supplies and services as printing, mailings, stationery, and gift-plates. Some substantial donations have been made specifically to cover such operating expenses, which have also included design and printing of gift-plates to be used for significant donations to the library's special collections.

11. Friends on the State and National Level

by

W. LYLE EBERHART

VIRGINIA S. HEINEMANN

SANDY DOLNICK

ROGER H. PARENT

A state Friends group should be the communicating link between libraries, their communities, and the state. It should strive for closer understanding and cooperation between citizens and their libraries. It should encourage the formation of new Friends groups, providing information and assistance. It should stimulate existing Friends groups to wider and deeper activity through the directors and with the awards. Most important, it should work to establish good relations throughout the state between the local Friends groups, the libraries, trustees, and the state and national library organizations.

A PERSPECTIVE FOR THE '80s FROM THE STATE

From the vantage point of the state, Friends of the Library have only begun to tap the potential of the contributions they can make for the improvement of library services for all Americans. Friends groups in recent years have achieved significant levels of success in many communities. But the success stories, many of which are described in this volume, were satisfactory for the 70s; they will need to be extended into the less affluent 1980s if libraries are even to maintain their present level of services. Add to this the present deficiencies in and underfunding of library services, and there is an enormous challenge ahead for Friends groups. So long as the present trend to cut governmental spending as services continues, Friends have a special obligation to see that libraries receive their fair share of tax funds. In many communities and states, this is not happening. Since tax funds will not be completely adequate to support library services, Friends can help libraries secure gifts, bequests, and grants to sustain their programs. This trend, while national, can be resisted by action on the state and local level.

A relatively new development is for libraries, along with other educational agencies, to try to serve better those with special needs. American libraries for over one hundred years have developed programs for recent immigrants, for the unemployed, for those without convenient access to educational services. When library budgets are cut, special needs programs are sometimes lost first. Through public relations, through volunteer assistance in these programs, through the raising of special funds, Friends need to help libraries offer the best possible level of services to the handicapped and socially or economically deprived.

Inevitably, Friends fan out into their communities as representatives of libraries. Thus, there is a discrete body of public relations skills which can and should be learned by Friends. Personal influence at the state level remains the baseline of effective promotion of library services. The fact that the influence of Friends extends so naturally into governmental, business, and social concerns of the community greatly multiplies the influence of their efforts at library public relations. What libraries do well for different groups on the local level they can do as well and with greater effect on the state level.

Effective public relations efforts will continue to be central functions of Friends groups in the 1980s. Several fairly recent public opinion surveys indicate there has been little change in the low visibility of libraries and library services as far as the average citizen is concerned. Although the United States is characterized as an information society, relatively few are aware of the potential contributions libraries can make to such a society. It is especially on the state level that these widespread misperceptions must be addressed.

Statewide action by Friends is also justified by the emergence of larger units of service. Cooperative activity involving all kinds of libraries—academic, public, school, and special—will grow in the 1980s. Advances in computer and communications technology make it easier each year to share resources between different kinds of libraries, to the benefit of users of all libraries. Friends groups have usually been formed to aid one particular library. The trend toward interlibrary cooperation gives them the need to understand, advocate, and work for library resource sharing.

It is hoped that the 1980s will see a great growth in statewide Friends groups. Organized on such a basis, they can better cooperate with state library associations and agencies.
They can be more effective advocates for state library programs, legislation, and appropriations.

FORMING A STATEWIDE ORGANIZATION

If there are many Friends organizations in a state, they
may decide to form a statewide organization which acts as a
central agent for information and support in library matters.
A statewide Friends can reinforce existing groups and provide
the catalyst for the formation of new ones.

To start a state organization, representatives from existing local Friends should meet to determine the goals and functions of the proposed group and then to establish its working
structure. The base for membership should then be broadened
to include interested individuals and sponsoring organizations
or corporations.

In order to represent all parts of the state and to facilitate a personal relationship with the local groups, the executive board of the state group should include directors from
all areas of the state. Congressional districts are set up according to population/area distribution; they are a suggested
criterion for directorships. Each director can maintain contact with Friends in his or her area by attending some meetings. If new groups desire to form, a director is available
nearby to provide encouragement and assistance.

Friends of Wisconsin Libraries has been a strong and active
state group since it was founded in 1963. It is described below as a typical statewide Friends and the constitution and
bylaws of Friends of Wisconsin Libraries follow this description.

The executive officers—president, vice-president, secretary and treasurer—are elected to two-year terms. The executive board consists of these four officers, the immediate past-
president, nine directors elected to three-year terms and representing each congressional district in Wisconsin, and several directors-at-large appointed by the president. The executive board meets four or more times a year in locations around
the state. At these meetings, the general meetings and workshops are planned and administrative decisions are made.

Due to the geographic distances between members of the executive board, much work is done in committee. The legislative committee, through the newsletter or at the meetings,
keeps the members current on pending library-related legislation. The projects committee oversees publications that as-

sist in forming new Friends. The finance committee contacts foundations and corporations for memberships. The editor, with assistance from committees, is responsible for the newsletter. The National Library Week chairperson manages and judges a contest promoting that week and the activities committee manages and judges the Library of the Year award.

There are two meetings a year for the membership. The annual meeting is held in late April or early May. At this morning meeting elections are held, the Library of the Year award is presented, and business matters are brought before the group. A workshop or panel discussion follows the meeting. Next, there is a luncheon with a guest speaker. These annual meetings are held in libraries at the invitation of local groups that wish to show off their new library or an addition to their present library.

The other membership meeting is held in conjunction with the Wisconsin Library Association Conference in October. At this time a short business meeting is held and the National Library Week award is presented. The main emphasis is on workshops. These have discussed how to improve and publish newsletters, how to increase membership, and techniques of lobbying. After the workshop there is a joint luncheon with the Wisconsin Library Trustees Association, featuring a speaker secured by either the trustees or the Friends.

Friends of Wisconsin Libraries publishes a newsletter three or four times a year with news of local groups, information on future meetings and pending library legislation, and state news. A suggested way to keep up with the various groups in the state is to subscribe to a state news clipping service. In this way, the executive board can keep informed on local Friends activities and on the formation of new Friends groups.

The two contests sponsored each year have helped to generate interest. The Library of the Year award is based on activities and projects over one year, judged by activity reports submitted by local groups to a committee. All returns are compiled into a booklet and given to member groups as a membership incentive and to provide a network for idea exchange. The National Library Week award is presented to the group with the most innovative and/or successful Library Week promotion.

CONSTITUTION AND BYLAWS OF FRIENDS OF WISCONSIN LIBRARIES

Article I.   NAME. The name of this organization shall be "Friends of Wisconsin Libraries."

Article II.   PURPOSE. The purposes shall be to foster

closer relations between Wisconsin libraries and citizens of Wisconsin; to promote knowledge of the Library's functions, resources, services and needs; to aid in the development of a program for the extension and improvement of the library services and resources. The purposes are exclusively educational and charitable and no substantial part of the activities may ever be to influence legislation by propaganda or otherwise. In the event of dissolution all assets will be distributed for exclusively educational and charitable purposes.

Article III.   MEMBERSHIP.
Section 1. Membership in this organization shall be open to all individuals in sympathy with its purposes.
Section 2. Each organization and individual member shall be entitled to one vote.
Section 3. Each year, those persons who are serving on the Wisconsin Committee for National Library Week shall be honorary members of this organization.

Article IV.   OFFICERS.
Section 1. The governing body of this organization shall be an executive board composed of one member from each Wisconsin Congressional District, a state-wide member-at-large, and the five officers as provided for in Section 2 of this article. Each Board member except for the five officers shall be elected for a three-year term except that at the first election the members selected from the First, Second, and Third Districts shall be for a one-year term, those from the Fourth, Fifth, and Sixth Districts shall be for a two-year term, and those from the Seventh, Eighth, and Ninth Districts and the member-at-large shall be for a three-year term. Thereafter, the terms of all members of the governing body who are not officers shall be for three years.

If a member of the governing body is unable to attend one of the meetings, he shall appoint his alternate to attend in his place, and this alternate shall be a voting member of the meeting.

In addition, the Board may provide from time to time for such ex officio members as they deem advisable.

Section 2. This organization shall have the following officers: President, Vice-President, Secretary, and Treasurer, and the terms of the officers will be for two years. The officers shall constitute the Executive Committee.

Section 3. The terms of the Board members and of the officers shall commence on May 1 of each year, with the first year commencing May 1, 1963.

Section 4. The first Board members and the first officers shall be elected by the Steering Committee created to form this organization, and said committee may elect any citizens of the State of Wisconsin they deem interested in the purposes of this organization. All successive elections to the Board and officers shall be made by the membership of this organization at the annual meeting to be held in April of each year. At each annual meeting, the organization shall elect successors for the Board members whose terms expire on May 1 of that year and in each odd-numbered year shall also elect the officers of the organization.

Section 5. Officers shall be elected at the annual meeting by a majority vote. A nominating committee, appointed by the President, shall submit a slate of candidates, and nominations may be made from the floor.

Section 6. Any vacancies on the Board or among the officers due to an unexpired term shall be filled by the Board, and such appointment shall be for the length of the term vacated.

Article V.   DUTIES OF OFFICERS

Section 1. The officers shall have the usual duties and authority exercised by officers of a non-profit corporation.

Article VI.   COMMITTEES

Section 1. The Board may appoint committees as they deem advisable with necessary powers and authorities. The persons serving on committees may be either Board members or other members of the organization.

Article VII.   MEETINGS

Section 1. The Board shall hold at least two meetings a year.

Section 2. This organization shall hold its annual meeting in the month of April, for handling of organization business and elections. Members shall be notified in writing at least two weeks prior to the date of the meeting.

Section 3. Special meetings of the Board may be called by the President or upon the request of any three members of the Board. The President or the members of the Board desiring to call a special meeting shall make application to the Secretary, and the Secretary shall give at least one week's notice of said meeting in writing.

Section 4. A special meeting of the organization may be called at any time by the Board.

Article VIII.   DUES. Dues shall be payable annually and shall become due on the last day of April. There shall be three classes of dues:

1. Individual Membership $3.00
2. Organization Membership   7.00
3. Supporting Membership   15.00 and up

Article IX.   FISCAL YEAR. The fiscal year shall run from May 1 to April 30. All funds shall be deposited to the account of the Friends of Wisconsin Libraries and shall be disbursed by the Treasurer as authorized by the Executive officers or the Board.

Article X.   DISTRIBUTION OF ASSETS UPON DISSOLUTION. Upon the dissolution of the corporation, the entire net assets remaining after the payment or satisfaction of any and all liabilities and obligations of the corporation shall be distributed to such organization or organizations organized and operated exclusively for charitable, educational, religious, or scientific purposes as shall at the time qualify as an exempt organization or organizations under Section 501(c)(3) of the Internal Revenue Code of 1954 (or the corresponding provision of any future United States Internal Revenue Law), or to the federal government, or to a state or local government, for a public purpose, as the Board of Directors shall determine.

Article XI.   AMENDMENTS. Amendments to this Constitution and Bylaws may be made at any meeting of the general membership by a two-thirds vote of those present, provided that notice of the proposed amendment has been given to all members at least a week before the meeting.

Article XII.   PARLIAMENTARY PROCEDURE. Robert's Rules of Order, Revised, when not in conflict with these Bylaws and Constitution, shall govern the proceedings of this organization and of the Board.

AMENDMENTS

Article IV.   OFFICERS
Section 2. This organization shall have the following officers: President, Vice-president, Secretary, Treasurer and the Immediate Past President. The terms of the President and the Secretary shall be two years commencing in May of the odd-numbered years. The terms of the Vice-president and the Treasurer shall be two years commencing in May of the even-numbered years. The officers shall constitute the Executive Committee.

Article VII.   MEETINGS
Section 2. This organization shall hold its annual meeting in the week following National Library Week for handling of organization business and elections. . . .

FRIENDS NATIONWIDE

Friends groups, because they are representative of library users, give important feedback to libraries and the institutions that direct them. They share with the American Library Association the goals of supporting library service. Friends groups and ALA have cooperated since the 1950s in this support. More recently, Friends of Libraries USA has been formed as a national association of Friends, which allows the sharing of information among themselves.

FRIENDS AS REPRESENTATIVES OF PUBLIC INTERESTS

Appropriating authorities are closely scrutinizing the performance and effectiveness of libraries which compete, not always successfully, with other tax-supported organizations for limited financial resources. During the past decade, those who fund libraries have changed their emphasis from providing more and more dollars to examining the results of these investments.

As library effectiveness is examined by funding agencies, libraries must prove that they are responding to local needs. In order to do this, libraries must develop comprehensive plans of service based on specific local needs. Assessing these local needs and devising innovative means of fulfilling them are the principal tasks facing libraries today. All those who are concerned about library service—trustees, Friends, librarians, civic leaders, library users, and nonusers—are needed to help in this effort.

Friends are traditionally representative of the different groups which make up library users. They are aware of special needs, concerns, pressures, and restraints affecting libraries, as well as resources and strengths in communities. Friends can be an influential force for identifying needs and urging any needed change. This characteristic they share with ALA. Both want to promote quality, user-oriented library service at the local, regional, and national level. They both want libraries to deliver information effectively. The importance and contributions of Friends in pursuit of this goal is recognized by ALA, who consistently supports the activities of Friends groups. This support is given through the Library Administration and Management Association (LAMA), a division of ALA in which many of the member librarians are concerned with interpreting programs to the community.

THE AMERICAN LIBRARY ASSOCIATION

The American Library Association, which was founded in 1876, is the oldest and largest library association in the world. Its membership is composed of more than thirty-five thousand librarians; library trustees; authors; organizations which are concerned about libraries (such as publishers); and Friends of libraries in the United States, Canada, and abroad. Together these groups work to make ALA one of the most influential factors in the development and growth of library service.

ALA has its national headquarters in Chicago and maintains an office in Washington, D.C., where librarians educate and work with legislators to obtain the necessary government support for libraries. Through the Washington office, ALA secures federal funds for library facilities, programs, media training, research, and construction of every type of library.

ALA is also involved in maintaining an intellectual freedom program and defends the library's right to shelve and circulate materials without restriction, encourages libraries to challenge censorship, and supports everyone's right to read. These activities embody the philosophy of ALA's Library Bill of Rights, which serves as the library's interpretation of the First Amendment of the U.S. Constitution.

ALA promotes libraries through its Public Information Office, which produces graphics, news releases, and related materials, and places public service ads with national magazines and the networks. It generates enthusiasm, greater public recognition, and support of libraries. National Library Week is one part of ALA's year-round public service advertising effort.

ALA sets standards and guidelines to meet the rapidly changing needs of the public that libraries serve. ALA stimulates achievement in various fields such as publishing, library architecture, and public relations through its awards programs. Perhaps the best known of the ALA awards are the Newbery and Caldecott Medals, which recognize superior quality in children's literature.

FRIENDS AND ALA

ALA supports the activities of Friends groups both through the Friends of Libraries Committee of LAMA (formerly the Library Administration Division) and through publications. The Friends of Libraries Committee was founded in 1957. This committee, through the office of the LAMA Executive Secretary at ALA, provides Friends groups throughout the country with materials, information, and advice that help to improve their local organization and its services and programs.

The Friends of Libraries Committee has also produced many programs and activities at ALA annual Conferences. The Friends luncheons have been among the most noteworthy events at each Conference. These luncheons have raised the level of awareness among the more than ten thousand annual Conference participants that Friends provide libraries with vital support. These luncheons also draw libraries, library issues, and Friends to the attention of the public by inviting nationally known figures to address the attendees. The Friends of Libraries Committee also hosts information workshops at each Conference. Frequently programs are held on such topics as establishing Friends groups in public or academic libraries, program planning, and the political process.

ALA publications include indispensable tools of the library profession, journals, monographs, reference works, and lists of notable books in many fields. In 1962 ALA published *Friends of the Library: Organization and Activities*, by Sarah Leslie Wallace. This book, now outdated, described Friends groups of different sizes and types and the activities of these groups. In 1978 ALA, through its Friends of Libraries Committee, Public Relations Section, Library Administration Division, published *A Directory of Friends of the Libraries Groups in the United States*, compiled by Sandy Dolnick. This directory has been a major source of information for Friends groups throughout the country. It includes more than 2,100 entries divided by geographic area and includes all types of libraries. It was also LAMA that began quarterly publication of *Friends of the Library National Notebook,* now the official newsletter of Friends of Libraries USA.

FRIENDS OF LIBRARIES USA

As the rate of growth of Friends of the Library groups accelerated in the late 1970s, it became clear that some structure was called for to increase communication and visibility for Friends.

The first attempt at forming some link among existing groups was the publication in 1978 of the aforementioned *Friends of the Library National Notebook*. The seven hundred subscribers surpassed all expectations; they included individuals, libraries, and organized Friends groups in both large and small academic and public libraries. As further contacts were made, it became clear that more information and a continuing program of education were needed.

Consequently, Friends of Libraries USA was founded in 1979. The new group provides access to information and ideas for library support groups of all sizes, and all types of libraries. As an educational and advocacy group in support of better library service, it stimulates and encourages grass roots advocacy, disseminating information with help from the ALA Washington office. It also became the publisher of the *Friends of the Library National Notebook* in 1979.

Friends of Libraries USA helps members formulate public relations efforts, publicize their existence and the services they perform. Friends of Libraries USA is also planning regional meetings to get more groups involved.

The group's office is in ALA headquarters in Chicago. Its meetings are held at ALA Midwinter Conferences and June Conferences in various parts of the country. Its board of directors represents academic and public libraries from all over the United States.

The *Friends of Libraries National Notebook* has become the official means of communication for the group. Its circulation is now about 3,500. Its most popular feature is a compendium of activities called "Friends in Action," which details, in each issue, forty to sixty programs held by various groups. The name, city, and state of each group is given so it can be contacted for further information. Other columns include program ideas and book reviews, and materials for sale by and for Friends.

The dues scale for Friends of Libraries USA is based on the size of the group, and is also available for individuals, clubs and associations, and corporations. The Friends of Libraries USA is incorporated as a tax-exempt, nonprofit organization.

The structure of this umbrella type organization provides a back-up, where none existed previously, for Friends of Library groups, library associations, and individuals. The very quality that makes a Friends group so valuable to their library—its interest in the particular institution rather than all libraries—makes it difficult for most Friends of the Library to see their role outside their own community. Yet it is evident by the descriptions in this chapter how necessary it is for Friends to enlarge their interest area.

LOOKING AHEAD

The voice of the citizen is often heeded by politicians, and the more Friends realize their influence the more they will be appreciated by the library community. The voice of the Friends is often overlooked by professionals at the local and state levels—not deliberately but because few mechanisms exist that give this interest group a chance to express their interest and their opinions.

Some enlightened states are seeking to involve Friends as part of citizen-trustee councils, and this can only be seen as a positive step. State library associations and state divisions for library service need to learn to include Friends in their meetings, so that an educated group will exist well before the last budget meeting is held, and the cry for citizen input is heard. One of the overwhelming lessons learned from the White House Conference was that the public was not adequately informed about library systems.

Friends exist to help their libraries, and as is evidenced by the material in this book, will use every means within their power to do so. It is up to libraries to assist the Friends in this effort. It takes two to form a partnership, and it takes the library profession and citizens together to make Friends of and for the library.

Friends Group Survey

AMERICAN LIBRARY ASSOCIATION
Library Administration Division
Public Relations Section
Friends of Libraries Committee

Name of Friends Group_____

Name of Library_____

Address_____
          Street   City   State   Zip

(Please circle the answer code that applies or supply the
   information requested.)

1. a. Which category best describes
      your library?   Academic...................1
                              Public....................2
                              Other, specify_____3

   b. Is this the main library?   Yes_____
                              No_____

2. Is your library unionized?   Professionals Yes........1
                                           No.........2

                              Non-
                              Professionals Yes........1
                                           No.........2

                              Maintenance   Yes........1
                                           No.........2

3. How large is the area your
   library serves?   Miles_____
                              Population_____
                              Size of collection_____
                              Size of budget_____

4. a. In what year was the Friends
      Group organized?   _____

   b. Has it been continually
      active?   Yes_____
                                         No_____

   c. Who organized the Friends
      Group?   Trustees...................1
                                         Community organizations,
                                         specify_____2
                                         Citizens...................3
                                         Alumni.....................4
                                         Other, specify_____5

5. a. Does the Friends Group have
      tax-exempt status for
      federal tax?   Yes.........1
                                                     No..........2

   b. For state tax?   Yes.........1
                                                     No..........2

6. a. Does your Friends Group have
      dues?   Yes......................1
                                         No (Skip to Q7)...........2
      (If Yes)
   b. What are the dues for each
      membership category?

                        Individual $_____
                        Couple   _____
                        Family   _____
                        Sustaining   _____
                        Patron   _____
                        Benefactor   _____
                        Life   _____
                        Corporate   _____
                        Student   _____
                        Other, specify _____

   c. What was your paid membership
      on April 1, 1977?_____

7. a. How do you communicate with
      your members?_____

   b. If one of the means is a
      newsletter...

      1) Is it sent out on...   A regular basis?..........1
                                       An irregular basis?.......2

2) Approximately how many issues per year are put out? _____

3) Who writes and edits the
newsletter?   Library staff.............1
                           Volunteers................2
                           Other, specify_____3

8. a. Are there any paid employees
working for the Friends Group? Yes......................1
                                No (Skip to Q9)..........2
   (If Yes)
   b. Who pays the salaries?   Friends Group.............1
                                 Library...................2
                                 Other, specify_____3

   c. What is the total number of
   hours per month worked by
   paid employees?   Full Time   Part Time

                                _____   _____

   d. On a separate sheet of paper, please describe briefly the
   important duties of each employee.

9. a. Does your Friends Group do
   any lobbying?   Yes......................1
                                No (Skip to Q10)..........2
   (If Yes)
   b. With what legislative groups
   do the Friends lobby?   Federal government........1
                                State government..........2
                                Local government..........3
                                Other, specify_____4

   c. Do the Friends belong to a
   legislative network?   Yes......................1
                                No.......................2

   d. In what ways does the
   Friends Group lobby?_____

   _____

10. a. Do the Friends engage in any
    other political activities? Yes......................1
                                 No (Skip to Q11)..........2
    (If Yes)
    b. Please describe the other
    activities:_____

    _____

11. a. Do the Friends perform any
      specific services for the
      library?   Yes........................1
                                        No (Skip to Q12)..........2
      (If Yes)
   b. Please list and describe
      the specific services the
      Group performs:_____

      _____

      _____

   c. Which of these services
      has proven successful?_____

      _____

      _____

12. a. List the programs the
      Friends sponsored during
      the last membership year:_____

      _____

      _____

   b. Who organizes the
      programs?   Friends Group............1
                                       Library..................2
                                       Other, specify_____3

   c. Does your Friends Group
      work with other community
      organizations to sponsor
      Programs?   Yes........................1
                                       No (Skip to Q13)..........2
      (If Yes)
   d. List the community organiza-
      tions the Friends worked with
      during the last membership
      year:_____

      _____

      _____

13. a. Do you work with a profession-
      al fund raiser?   Yes........................1
                                       No.........................2

   b. Please describe the ways you
      raise funds, the amounts

generated from each activity,
and the total amount of funds
raised in one year, using a
separate sheet of paper if
necessary_____

_____

_____

c. What are the purposes for
which funds are raised?_____

_____

_____

d. How is recognition given to
donors?_____

_____

_____

e. What are the criteria for
allocating funds?_____

_____

_____

14. a. How do you conduct your membership drive? (Use a separate
sheet of paper if necessary):_____

_____

_____

b. What incentives do you have
for membership?_____

_____

_____

15. a. Does a member of the library
staff serve as a liaison to
the Friends?   Yes.....................1

(If Yes)   No (Skip to Q16).........2

b. What is the title of the
library staff member who is
the liaison?   _____
                                         Title

16. a. Do the Friends have a repre-
       sentative on the Library's
       Board of Trustees?   Yes (Skip to Q17)..........1
                                    No.........................2
       (If No)
    b. Is there input from the
       Friends to the Board?   Yes........................1
                                    No.........................2

17. a. Is the library director
       personally involved with
       the Friends?   Yes........................1
                                    No (Skip to end)...........2
       (If Yes)
    b. Please describe the nature
       of the involvement:_____

       _____

       _____

18. a. Who writes the news re-
       leases for your Group?   Member.....................1
                                    Library staff..............2
                                    PR firm....................3

    b. What are your most success-
       ful public relations efforts
       in terms of making the pub-
       lic aware of your Group?_____

       _____

       _____

    c. What generates the most news
       coverage?_____

       _____

       _____

19. a. Does your Group belong to
       your State Friends Group?   Yes........................1
                                    No.........................2
                                    Does not apply_____

    b. Does a representative of
       your Group belong to the
       American Library Association?
                                    Yes........................1
                                    No.........................2

    c. Would your group be inter-
       ested in being a member of
       a national organization of
       Library Friends, if it were
       to be organized, to continue
       sharing our mutual concerns? Yes........................1
                                       No.........................2

20. What areas are you especially
    interested in having discussed
    in the book for Friends of the
    Library?_____

    _____

    _____

21. a. What have been the chief
       accomplishments of your
       Friends organization?_____

      _____

      _____

    b. What have been the major
       benefits to the library?   Fundraising................1
                               Acquisition of special
                               collections materials......2
                               Development of community
                               support for the library....3
                               Other......................4

22. a. From your experience what
       are the greatest obstacles
       in organizing and running
       a Friends Group?   Relationship with pro-
                               fessional staff............1
                               Lack of volunteer help.....2
                               Lower priority in com-
                               munity than other volun-
                               teer service groups........3
                               Other......................4

    b. We promise anonymity—
       please detail your expe-
       rience; it may be of great
       help to others:_____

      _____

      _____

23. We plan to reproduce various forms necessary for the func-
    tioning of a Friends Group in the appendix to the book. If
    possible, please send us copies of the following:

    _____Titles of Officers and committee chairpeople and/or
          governing board

    _____Constitution and Bylaws

    _____Newsletter

    _____Membership brochure

    _____Other

    The materials not used will be kept on file at ALA Head-
    quarters.

24. Please add your comments, if any:_____

    _____

    _____

    _____

    _____

    _____

    _____

    Name of person responding:_____

    Position in Friends Group:_____

    Phone number:_____
                  (Area Code)

                              THANK YOU!

Please send completed form to: Mrs. Sandy Dolnick
                                 4909 North Ardmore Avenue
                                 Milwaukee, WI 53217

Friends of the Library Respondents

Alabama
   Carnegie Library of Selma
   Emmet O'Neal Library
   Huntsville-Madison County
     Public Library
   Scottsboro Public Library
Arizona
   Sierra Vista Municipal
     Library
Arkansas
   Central Arkansas Library
     System
California
   Alpine Library
   Bancroft Library
   Berkeley Public Library
   Fallbrook Library
   Napa City-County Library
   Oakhurst Branch, Madera
     County Library
   Palm Springs Library
   Palo Alto City Library
   Sacramento Public Library
   San Francisco Public
     Library
   Santa Barbara Public
     Library

   Stanford University
     Libraries
   University of California,
     San Diego Libraries
   University of California,
     Santa Barbara Library
   Whittier Public Library
Colorado
   Cortez Public Library
   Denver Public Library
   Lamar Public Library
   Littleton Library and Museum
     (Edwin A. Bemis Public Li-
     brary)
   Pitkin County Library
   University of Colorado,
     Boulder Library
   Westminster Public Library
Connecticut
   Bethany Library
   East Hampton Public Library
   Greenwich Library
   Groton Public Library
   Ledyard Library
   New Haven Free Public Library
   Ridgefield Library
   Somers Public Library

Southbury Public Library
West Hartford Library
Yale University
Delaware
Concord Pike
Florida
Bradford County Public
    Library
Cape Coral Public Library
Clearwater Public Library
Cocoa Beach Public Library
Collier County Free Public
    Library
Cooper Memorial Public
    Library
De Soto County Public
    Library
Deland Free Public Library
Dunedin Public Library
Elsie Quirk Public Library
Englewood Charlotte Public
    Library
Florida State University
    Library
Fort Lauderdale Branch,
    Broward County Library
Gulf Beaches Public
    Library, Inc.
Gulfport Public Library
Jacksonville Public
    Library
Lauderdale Lakes Branch,
    Broward County Library
Maitland Public Library
Martin County Library
Melbourne Public Library
North Port Library
Orange Park Branch of the
    Clay County Library Sys-
    tem
Orlando Public Library
Pensacola Public Library
Plantation Library
Port Charlotte Library
Satellite Beach Public
    Library
Taylor County Library

Georgia
Atlanta Public Library
Emory University Library
Idaho
Boise Public Library
Madison County Library
Illinois
Arlington Heights Memorial
    Library
Decatur Public Library
Evans Public Library
Flossmoor Public Library
Hinsdale Public Library
Northwestern University
    Library
Rock Island Public Library
Rolling Meadows Library
Staunton Public Library
University of Illinois
    Library
Warren/Newport Public
    Library
Waukegan Public Library
Indiana
Gary Public Library
Knightstown Public Library
Monroe County Public
    Library
Willard Library of
    Evansville, Indiana
Iowa
Carlisle Library
Carroll Public Library
University of Iowa
    Libraries
Kansas
Emporia Public Library
Goodland Public Library
Wichita Public Library
Kentucky
Lexington Public Library
Louisville Free Public
    Library
Paul Sawyier Library
Louisiana
LSU Library
Magale Library

Tulane University Library
Maine
Brunswick Public Library
Falmouth Memorial Library
Prince Memorial Library
Maryland
Catonsville Area Branch of
the Baltimore County
Library
Talbot County Free Library
Massachusetts
Belmont Public Library
Bridgewater Public Library
Chester C. Corbin Public
Library
Fall River Public Library
Framingham Public Libraries
Hudson Public Library
J. V. Fletcher Library
Lawrence Library
Libraries of Boston
University
Memorial Hall Library
Merriam-Gilbert Public
Library
New Bedford Free Public
Library
Northborough Free Library
Salisbury Public Library
Stoneham Public Library
Swampscott Public Library
University of Massachusetts
Watertown Free Public
Library
Worcester Public Library
Michigan
Ann Arbor Public Library
Detroit Public Library
Minnesota
Albert Lea Public Library
Augsburg Park Community
Library, Hennepin County
System
Champlin Community Library
Eden Prairie Community
Library
Edian Community Library
Excelsior Community Library

Granite Falls Public
Library
Great River Regional
Library
Hopkins Community Library,
Hennepin County System
Long Lake Library,
Hennepin County System
Medina Community Library
Minneapolis Public Library
Osseo Community Library
Penn Lake Library
Rochester Public Library
Rockford Road Community
Library
St. Louis Park Community
Library
Wabasha Public Library
Westonka Community Library
Mississippi
Gulfport-Harrison County
Jackson County Libraries
Margaret Reed Crosby
Memorial Library
Missouri
University City Public
Library
University of Missouri-
Kansas City Libraries
University of Missouri
Library and the State
Historical Society Library
Montana
Daniels County Free Library
Gallatin Libraries
Livingston Public Library
Missoula Public Library
Nebraska
Lincoln City Libraries
Omaha Public Library
Nevada
Douglas County Public
Library
Ormsby Public Library
New Hampshire
Amherst Town Library
Dartmouth College Library
Richards Free Library

Rye Public Library
Windham Library
New Jersey
Bloomfield Public Library
Bridgeton Free Public
Library
East Orange Public Library
Fairfield Public Library
Franklin Lakes Public
Library
Ho-Ho-Kus Public Library
Little Silver Public
Library
Marie Fleche Memorial
Library
Metuchen Public Library
Middletown Township
Library
Princeton Public Library
Riverton Free Library
Springfield Free Public
Library
Wayne Public Library
Westville Free Public
Library
New Mexico
Alamogordo Public Library
Albuquerque Public Library
Hobbs Public Library
New York
Bethpage Public Library
Buffalo and Erie County
Public Library
Chappaqua Library
Clinton Hill Branch of the
Brooklyn Public Library
Columbia University
Libraries
Cornell University
Libraries
Farmingdale Public Library
Fayetteville Free Library
Freeport Memorial Library
Greenwich Free Library
Hampton Bays Public
Library
Hicksville Public Library
Hillside Public Library

Long Beach Public Library
Manhasset Public Library
North Merrick Public
Library
North Syracuse Free Library
Oyster Bay—East Norwich
Public Library
Port Washington Public
Library
Saratoga Springs Public
Library
Seaford Public Library
Syracuse University
Libraries
Town of Tonawanda Public
Library
University of Rochester
Libraries
Waterford Public Library
North Carolina
Library of Asheville
Cumberland County Public
Library
Duke University Library
Greensboro Public Library
Union County Public Library
University of North Caro-
lina—Chapel Hill
Ohio
Library of Canfield
Cleveland Public Library
Franklin Sylvester Library
Granville Public Library
Greenford Public Library
Hutton Memorial Library
Marion Public Library
Miami University Libraries
North Branch Public Library
of Youngstown Makoning
County
Ohio State University
Libraries
Pickaway County District
Public Library
Poland Branch of the Public
Library of Youngstown
Stow Public Library

Oklahoma
  Pryor Public Library
  Tulsa Public Library
Pennsylvania
  Abington Township Public
    Library
  Allentown Public Library
  Bethany Public Library
  Butler Public Library
  Columbia Public Library
  Erie City and County
    Library
  Lancaster County Library
  Lebanon Community Library
  McKeesport Carnegie Free
    Library
  Samuel W. Smith Memorial
    Public Library
  Scranton Public Library
  Susquehanna County
    Historical Society and
    Free Library Association
  Swarthmore Public Library
Rhode Island
  Library of Brown University
  Pawtucket Public Library
South Carolina
  Cherokee County Public
    Library
  Hilton Head Island Branch,
    Beaufort County Library
  Richland County Public
    Library
Tennessee
  Gorham MacBane Library
  Knoxville-Knox County
    Public Library
  Memphis/Shelby County
    Library
Texas
  Amarillo Public Library
  Austin Public Library
  Bailey H. Dunlap Memorial
    Library
  Batt Holdsworth Memorial
    Library
  Beaumont Public Libraries
  Dallas Public Library

Dawson County Public
    Library
  Deer Park Public Library
  East Side Branch, Waco-
    McLennan County Library
  Ector County Library
  Fondren Library at Rice
    University
  Fort Worth Public Library
  Houston Public Library
  Kenedy Public Library
  Kountze Public Library
  Lucy Hill Patterson
    Memorial Library
  McKinney Memorial Public
    Library
  Plano Public Library
  Portland Public Library
  Rosenberg Library
  Seguin-Guadalupe County
    Public Library
  Sherman Public Library
  South Waco Branch, Waco-
    McLennan County Library
  Texas A&M University
    Libraries
  University of Houston
    Libraries
  Waco-McLennan County
    Library
Vermont
  Ilsley Library
  Kellogg-Hubbard Library
  Waterbury Public Library
Virginia
  Buchanan County Public
    Library
  Central Rappahannock
    Regional Library
  Fauquier County Public
    Library
  Jefferson Madison Regional
    Library
  Portsmouth Public Library
  Redford Public Library
  Richmond Public Library
  Virginia Beach Public
    Library

Washington
   Bainbridge Island Branch,
      Kitsap Regional Library
   Lakes District Library
   Olympia Public Library
   Tacoma Community College
      Library
West Virginia
   Kingwood Public Library
   Martinsburg-Berkeley
      County Public Library
   Morgantown Public Library
   Ravenswood Branch, Jackson
      County Public Library
Wisconsin
   Appleton Public Library
   Berlin Public Library
   Brookfield Public Library
   Brown County Library
   Cedarburg Public Library
   Door County Libraries

E. U. Demmer Memorial
   Library
Jefferson Library
Kenosha Public Library
Madison Public Library
McMillan Memorial Library
Mead Public Library
Milwaukee Public Library
New Berlin Public Library
New Holstein Public Library
Ripon Public Library
University of Wisconsin-
   Madison Libraries
Waukesha Public Library
Wauwatosa Public Library
Williams Free Library
Wyoming
   Lincoln County Library
   Sheridan County-Fulmer
      Library

Constitution, Friends of the Library, University of Massachusetts (Amherst)

As Adopted by the Trustees at the First Annual Meeting of November 15, 1970, and Incorporating Amendments Ratified by Trustees and Members 'at the Third Annual Meeting, October 29, 1972

I   The name of the organization shall be: Friends of the Library, University of Massachusetts (Amherst).

II The purpose of the organization shall be the enrichment of the total resources and facilities of the University of Massachusetts Library.

III Membership shall be open to any individual, business firm, or group interested in the objectives of the Friends.

IV Annual membership contributions shall be receivable in the University of Massachusetts Friends of the Library Trust Fund on or before December 31 of each year for the 12 succeeding months, according to the following schedule:

A	Student Member	$ 3
B	Contributing Member	10
C	Associate Member	25
D	Sustaining Member	50
E	Sponsoring Member	100
F	Patron	500

The first 4 categories are open to individuals only, and the last 2 are open to individuals or groups.

The Trustees may create, at their discretion, other appropriate categories of membership, and they may accept books or other materials needed by the Library in lieu of contributions in cash. All contributions to the University of Massachusetts Friends of the Library Trust Fund and gifts of materials to the Library are tax-deductible.

V   Gifts of materials or money which are offered subject to any conditions not specifically sanctioned by existing Library policy must be approved by the Director of Libraries. The Library assumes responsibility for administering expenditure of funds in accordance with the wishes expressed by the donors, for identifying materials given or purchased with gift bookplates or other suitable identification, and for sending acknowledgments to donors.

VI   All members of the Friends are welcome to use the Library's collections in any of its branches under prevailing regulations, and to avail themselves of such services as can be provided by Library staff. Members will also receive copies of the Library Newsletter and the Annual Report of the Friends. Each member is entitled to one vote in the annual election of the Trustees, and in such other matters as may require a vote of the members.

VII   Trustees of the Friends will serve initially at the invitation of the Temporary Faculty Trustees, for a period of two years, after which 12 Trustees shall be elected by the Membership for terms of one, two, and three years. In subsequent elections, Trustees will be elected for terms of three years to replace retiring members. In addition to twelve Trustees at large, three members shall be chosen by the University of Massachusetts Alumni Association, initially for terms of one, two, and three years, and thereafter, one Trustee is to be chosen every year for a term of three years. The University community shall be represented by the President of the Student Senate, the President of the Graduate Student Senate, and the chairman of the Faculty Senate Library Committee, each of whom is elected annually.

The Trustees shall act as an executive committee and shall annually elect a President, one or more Vice Presidents, a Treasurer, and a Secretary (or combine the last two functions in one officer). The Trustees shall have the power to conduct the affairs of the Friends, including the establishing of committees, the appointment or election of additional officers, and the filling of vacancies. The Chancellor of the University's Amherst campus and the Director of Libraries shall serve as ex-officio members of the Trustees and of all executive committees.

VIII   Annual meetings of the Friends shall be held at such time and place as may be determined by the Trustees, and other meetings at such times as may be deemed necessary or desirable. Six members shall constitute a quorum at any meeting of the Trustees or of the Membership.

IX   This constitution may be amended by a simple majority of those voting at the annual or any special meeting of the Membership; provided that at least 10 days prior to the vote notice of proposed amendments shall have been sent to all members. This constitution may also be amended by a majority vote of the Trustees provided that each Trustee has been notified of proposed amendments at least 10 days prior to the date of the meeting at which the vote is to be taken.

By-Laws of Friends of the Detroit Public Library, Inc.

ARTICLE I. MEMBERSHIP

Section 1. Any person or association interested in the objects of this corporation shall be eligible for membership upon the payment of dues.

Section 2. Membership in this corporation shall be of the following classes.

(a) MEMBER; upon the payment of Ten ($10.00) Dollars yearly dues.

(b) SUSTAINING MEMBER; upon the payment of Twenty-five ($25.00) Dollars yearly dues.

(c) AMICUS LIBRORUM MEMBER; upon the payment of Fifty ($50.00) Dollars yearly dues.

(d) PATRON MEMBER; upon the payment of One Hundred ($100.00) Dollars yearly dues.

(e) LIFE MEMBER; upon the payment of One Thousand ($1,000.00) Dollars in advance, which payment shall relieve the life member from any obligation to pay membership fees thereafter.

(f) HONORARY MEMBER; to be elected only by special action of the Board of Directors.

(g) CLUB OR ASSOCIATION MEMBER; upon the payment of Ten ($10.00) Dollars annually.

(h) COMMERCIAL OR INDUSTRIAL MEMBER; upon the payment of Fifty ($50.00) Dollars or more annually.

ARTICLE II. OFFICERS AND DIRECTORS

Section 1. The officers of this corporation shall consist of a President, a Vice President, a Secretary, an Assistant Secretary, a Treasurer, and an Assistant Treasurer, who shall be drawn from the members of this Corporation.

Section 2. Twenty-one (21) Directors shall be elected by the members of the Corporation as follows:

At each annual meeting, seven (7) Directors shall be elected to serve for a term of three (3) years.

In the event any director shall cease to be a member of the Corporation, he shall thereupon cease to be a director of the Corporation.

In addition, all past presidents of the Corporation shall become Honorary Directors and shall be invited to all regular and special meetings of the Board of Directors.

Section 3. The term of office of officers shall be for one (1) year, except that any officer shall serve until his successor has been duly elected and has qualified.

Section 4. The election of directors shall be by secret ballot; provided, however, that the members by majority vote at any regular called or specified annual meeting, may, as to any such meeting, waive the provisions of this section and elect directors by vote viva voce. Nominations for directors may be made from the floor at the time of the election; provided, however, that prior to the holding of any such election, the Board of Directors may, by majority vote, select a nominating committee to bring in recommendations for nominations for any and all offices to be filled. A majority vote of the members present shall be required to elect.

Section 5. The Director of the Detroit Public Library of Detroit, Michigan, shall at all times be a member of the Board of Directors; and in addition at each annual meeting the members shall elect an additional director to serve until the next annual meeting of the members. Such additional director shall be a member of the Detroit Library Commission.

ARTICLE III. DUTIES AND POWERS OF OFFICERS AND DIRECTORS

Section 1. The President shall preside at all meetings of the Corporation and of the Board of Directors. He shall ap-

point all standing and special committees, subject to the approval of the Board of Directors; and he shall be an ex-officio
member of such committees. The President shall call meetings
of the Board of Directors at such times he may deem advisable,
and shall call special meetings of the Board of Directors and/
or of the Corporation on the written request of not less than
three members of the Board. It shall be the duty of the President to carry out the will of the Board of Directors and of
the Corporation as expressed at their respective meetings, and
in general to conduct the affairs of the Corporation in a manner consistent with the authority and responsibility pertain-
ing to his office.

Section 2. In the absence of the President, or in the
event of his inability to act, the Vice President shall discharge the duties of the President.

Section 3. The Secretary shall give notice of all meetings of the Board of Directors and/or of the Corporation and
shall attend all such meetings and keep a true and accurate
record of all proceedings had thereat. The Secretary shall
keep a complete list of the names and addresses of all members
of the Corporation. He shall carry on the correspondence of
the Corporation as instructed by the Board of Directors and/or
by the President of the Corporation. The Assistant Secretary
shall assist the Secretary and shall discharge the duties of
the Secretary in the event of the Secretary's absence or inability to act.

Section 4. The Treasurer shall deposit all funds of this
Corporation to the account of the Friends of the Detroit Public Library, Inc., a Michigan non-profit corporation, in such
depositary and under such conditions as the Board of Directors
may, from time to time, direct. The Treasurer shall collect
all moneys due to this Corporation and shall keep an account
of all moneys received by and expended by or on behalf of this
Corporation and shall make disbursements only upon order of
the Board of Directors; provided, however, that as to such
funds as may from time to time be allocated by the Board of
Directors for the purchase of books or other materials for the
Detroit Public Library, such funds shall be disbursed by the
Treasurer upon the written order of the Librarian of the
Detroit Public Library of Detroit, Michigan. On leaving office,
either by limitation of his term of office or otherwise, the
Treasurer shall deliver to his successor all moneys, books,
papers and other property belonging to the Corporation which
may then be in his possession or under his custody or control,
and in the absence of or for want of such successor, he shall

deliver the same to the Secretary of the Board of Directors. In case of the absence or the inability of the Treasurer to act, the Board of Directors may authorize the President or any other one of the officers of the Corporation to issue checks or perform such other duties of the Treasurer as may in that event become necessary. All books, papers and other property in the custody of the Treasurer shall be kept by him in a safe place, to be approved by the Board of Directors. The Treasurer may at any time be required to give a bond in such sum as the Board of Directors may deem advisable; the cost of such bond to be paid out of the funds of the Corporation. The Treasurer's accounts shall be audited annually or as often as deemed necessary by the Board of Directors in such manner as may, from time to time, be determined by the Board.

Section 5. It shall be the duty of the Board of Directors to care for the property and interests of the Corporation and to determine policies for the conduct of its affairs. The Board of Directors shall have the power to raise and expend funds to promote the welfare of the Corporation and to employ any and all lawful means it may deem proper and expedient to secure the objects for which the Corporation is organized. The foregoing is subject always to the provisions of Article Five, Section Two.

Section 6. The Board of Directors shall meet within the State of Michigan and may meet as often and at such times and places as the Board may deem advisable; provided, however, the Board of Directors shall meet at least once every three months.

Section 7. The Board of Directors, by a majority vote of the directors present at any stated meeting, may at their option drop any director who has failed to attend three or more consecutive meetings of the Board without just cause, whereupon the director or directors so dropped shall immediately cease to be a director.

Section 8. The Board of Directors is authorized and empowered to fill any vacancy which may occur on the Board until the next election of the Corporation, and is hereby authorized and empowered to fill any vacancy in office for the balance of the unexpired term so filled.

Section 9. The Board of Directors may appoint committees, authorize sections and initiate other agencies which they, in their wise discretion, may deem reasonably necessary or appropriate to carry out the purposes of this corporation.

ARTICLE IV. MEETINGS OF THE CORPORATION

Section 1. The annual meeting of the Corporation shall be held not earlier than April 1 and not later than May 31, at the Detroit Public Library, Detroit, Michigan, or at such other place within the State of Michigan as the Board of Directors shall determine.

Section 2. Special meetings of the Corporation may be called by the President or by a majority of the Board of Directors whenever they shall deem a special meeting necessary or advisable. Special meetings shall also be called by the Secretary on the written request of not less than ten active members of the Corporation. In all cases of special meetings, the Secretary shall notify the entire membership of the Corporation not less than three (3) days before the time set for such special meeting, of the fact of the calling of such special meeting, of the time and place thereof, and of the purpose of such special meeting. The purpose of any special meeting must be stated in the call therefor.

Section 3. Directors of the Corporation shall be elected to fill any unfilled vacancies and to take the places of those whose terms are about to expire, at the annual meeting of the Corporation, immediately following which the new Board of Directors shall elect the officers for the ensuing year. Officers shall hold their respective offices for one year and/or until their successor or successors in office have been elected or appointed and have qualified by taking office.

Section 4. At the will of the President or of the majority of the Board of Directors, a special vote of the Corporation or of the Board of Directors may, at any time, be taken by mail on any matter except amendments to the BY-LAWS or the Articles of Incorporation, without the formality of calling or assembling a special meeting; provided, however, that no proposition submitted to the Corporation in this manner shall carry without a majority vote of the active members. Prerequisite to taking a vote under this Section, the Secretary shall mail a written ballot to each member and/or to each director, on each of which ballots shall be clearly stated the proposition or propositions to be voted upon and a distinct statement as to the date on or before which such ballot must be returned in order to be counted. Any decision made, as above provided, either by the Board of Directors or by the Corporation, shall have the same force and effect as if enacted at a regular convened meeting.

ARTICLE V. DUES AND DELINQUENCIES

Section 1. Dues for membership in this Corporation shall be in the amounts hereinabove set forth in Article 1 hereof.

Section 2. No member of this Corporation shall be liable except for unpaid dues, and no personal liability shall in any event attach to any member of this Corporation in connection with any of its undertakings, but all its liabilities shall be limited to its common funds and assets. Neither the Board of Directors nor the officers shall have any authority to borrow money or to incur any indebtedness or liability in the name of or on behalf of this Corporation. No member of the Board of Directors and no officer of this Corporation shall act as, or be deemed to be, agent of the members of this Corporation, or any of them, or have authority to incur any obligation whatsoever. No contract shall in any event be entered into and no obligation shall be incurred beyond the amount on hand or in bank, after deducting therefrom, or providing for, the total of all unpaid accounts and unpaid obligations and liabilities.

ARTICLE VI. QUORUMS AND PROXIES

Section 1. Five (5) directors, present in person, shall constitute a quorum at all meetings of the Board of Directors.

Section 2. Ten (10) members shall constitute a quorum at any meeting of the members of the Corporation, regular or special.

ARTICLE VII. AMENDMENTS

Section 1. These BY-LAWS may be amended at any meeting of the Corporation by a three-fourths (3/4) vote of the members present and voting, provided that notice of the proposed amendment is given in writing to all of the members at least ten (10) days before said meeting.

ARTICLE VIII. SALARIES AND EXPENSES

Section 1. All officers and directors, except, as hereinafter provided, shall serve without compensation, but the Board of Directors may authorize the disbursement of such necessary incidental expenses as may be properly incurred by officers or directors in the transaction of business of this Corporation, by way of reimbursement. In addition, the Board of Directors may authorize the payment as compensation for actual services rendered of a reasonable salary to the Secretary or to an Assistant Secretary whether or not such officer is also a director.

ARTICLE IX. RULES OF ORDER

Section 1. All meetings of the Corporation and of the Board of Directors shall be conducted in accordance with the latest revised edition of *Robert's Rules of Order*.

Approved September 24, 1942

Article I, Sections 2 and 3; Article II, Sections 1, 2 and 3; Article III, Section 3, amended January 31, 1945.

Article II, Section 2, par. 1; Article II, Section 2, par. 2, amended March 19, 1948.

Article I, Section 2, amended November 9, 1948.

Article I, Section 3; Article IV, Section 1; Article V, Section 1, amended January 19, 1949.

Article I, Section 2 (a); Article II, Section 2 and 5; Article IV, Section 3; Article VIII, Section 1, amended May 8, 1961.

Article II, Section 2, amended May 15, 1968.

Article I, Section 2 (a) deleted (c) deleted (i) amended May 18, 1971 (Annual membership meeting).

Article II, Sections 1 and 2, amended May 24, 1973 (Annual membership meeting).

Article II, Section 2, amended June 28, 1978 (Annual membership meeting).

June 1978

Contributors

Scott Bennett is Special Collections Consultant at the University of Illinois Library, Urbana. He has served as secretary-treasurer of their Friends and as editor of their annual publication, *Non Solus*. He is also a member of the Urbana Free Library Friends, and has served as a member of ALA's Friends of Libraries Committee.

Lillian M. Bradshaw is the Director of Libraries, Dallas, Texas. She has been associated with the Friends of the Dallas Public Library since their inception in 1950, and serves as their secretary. Besides her eminence in the library field, she has chaired ALA's Friends of Libraries Committee, and was on the advisory board and secretary of the Friends of Texas Libraries.

Gloria M. Comingore is presently serving as Secretary of the Friends of the Torrance Library in California. She has both chaired their book sale and served as newsletter editor. She is the author of a forty-nine page manual on book sales, which has been published by the Friends.

Sandy Dolnick is currently President of Friends of Libraries USA and edits *Friends of the Library National Notebook*. She has been active in Friends organizations in Wisconsin, has written articles on Friends, and was an official observer at the White House Conference on Library and Information Service.

Frances G. Donald is the Public Relations Director of the Greenwich, Connecticut, Library, and serves as staff liaison to the Friends. She is involved with their committees, including monthly gallery exhibits, Sunday concert series, membership drives, and special events. Publicity releases and printing for the Friends are handled through her office. She has served on ALA's Friends of Libraries Committee, and is a member of the Library Public Relations Council.

W. Lyle Eberhart is the Administrator for the Division of Library Services for the Wisconsin Department of Public Instruction. He has helped organize a public library Friends group, and served as the state library agency liaison to the Friends of Wisconsin Libraries. He is past president of the Association of State Library Agencies, and president-elect of the Chief Officers of State Library Agencies.

Joan Erwin, Coordinator of Community Relations for the Orlando, Florida, public library system, was promotion director at a public television station before assuming her present position. She serves as the library liaison with the Friends, attends all of their meetings, writes the Friends newsletter, issues their news releases, and maintains their mailing list and other files in her office.

Siegfried Feller is Chief Bibliographer and Associate Director for Collections and Resources at the University of Massachusetts Library, Amherst. He has been involved with the Friends since their inception, and now serves as secretary-treasurer. He is involved with the annual FOL sale, their annual meeting of trustees and members, and is a member of the nominating committee.

Karen Lynne Furlow is Corporate Librarian, J. Ray McDermott Co., Inc. She was on the planning committee for the Friends of the Library of Tulane, and was co-author of a *College and Research Libraries* article on Friends. She has been an active member of the ALA Friends of Libraries Committee.

Gloria Glaser is the Public Relations Director for the Nassau Library System, Uniondale, New York, and has been involved in organizing and developing Friends on a local and statewide level. She has organized institutes and workshops for Friends, and has been a spokeswoman for libraries in the media. She has served in many committee positions for the American Library Trustees Association.

Ann S. Gwyn, Head of the Special Collections Division of the Tulane University Library, New Orleans, was on the board of the planning group which formulated the Tulane Friends. She has served as liaison officer from the library to the Friends, organized a publication program with Friends' funds, and organized two Friends book sales.

Barbara R. Healy is Head of the Management Library at the University of Rochester, New York. She has served on the volunteers committee of the Rochester University Friends, and has been active on ALA's Friends of Libraries Committee.

Virginia S. Heinemann is President of the Friends of Wisconsin Libraries and has served as a trustee for the Marathon County public libraries. She was a delegate to the Governor's Conference on Library and Information Services and is a member of ALA's Friends of Libraries Committee.

Sarah C. Hite has served in numerous capacities, including president of the board of the Friends of the Denver Public Library. She has been an active member of ALA's Friends of Libraries Committee, and chairperson of the Trustees and Citizens Division of the Colorado Library Association. She was a delegate to the Governor's Conference on Libraries and Information Services. She received much of her training in Management by Objectives through the Junior League.

Andrea L. Hynes is the Area Librarian, Pierce County Library, Tacoma, Washington. She has served as staff liaison between the Friends and the Bonney Lake Branch Library, meeting with the Friends and coordinating their activities and programs with the library district. She is currently working with three Friends of the Library groups in the district.

B. J. Jahnke is the Assistant Librarian/Coordinator of Children's Services at the Evanston Public Library. She was formerly their coordinator of community services. She has served as a member of ALA's Friends of Libraries Committee.

Kenneth A. Lohf is the Librarian for Rare Books and Manuscripts, Columbia University. He serves as secretary-treasurer to the Friends of the Columbia Libraries, and as managing editor of the *Columbia Library Columns*.

Caroline A. Loose is the Principal of the J. Curtin School, Milwaukee, Wisconsin. She has served as consultant to schools instituting a library program or developing an in-house library. She served on the board of The Bookfellows, Friends of the Milwaukee Public Library, and was both program chairperson and first vice-president.

Anne J. Mathews is Associate Professor and Director of Continuing Education, Graduate School of Librarianship and Information Management, University of Denver. She is a member of the board of managers, Friends of the Denver Public Library and of the board of directors, Friends of Libraries USA, and was involved in the formation of a Friends of Colorado Libraries Roundtable while president of the Colorado Library Association.

Hazel B. Maxwell served as President of the board of trustees of the Milwaukee Public Library for many years, and was active in state and national trustee organizations. She has been a member of The Bookfellows, Friends of the Milwaukee Public Library.

Elizabeth Mozley is the Executive Secretary of the Syracuse, New York, University Library Associates. She is the coordinator of all of the activities of the associates and editor of their publication, *The Courier*. She has also served as a trustee in public library systems.

Roger H. Parent is the Executive Secretary of LAMA and ex officio secretary of Friends of Libraries USA. At the Mercantile Library Association in New York City, he organized a group of volunteers that sponsored author lectures and book discussion groups, and edited their newsletter.

Paul T. Scupholm serves as the Executive Secretary of the Friends of the Detroit Public Library. He is the first full-time employee of a Friends organization, and has helped the group in a variety of ways.

Marvin H. Stone is the Librarian for Fine Collections at the Dallas Public Library. As rare books librarian (rare books are a special project of the Dallas Friends) and library representative to the Friends, he has attended most board and general membership meetings of the Friends for the last ten years. He also has assisted with the newsletters, membership campaigns, and book shows sponsored by the Friends.

Mrs. Betty Tholen is a member of the board of trustees of the Emporia Public Library, Kansas. She has served as president of the Emporia Friends and was on their initial organizing committee. She has assisted in the formation of groups throughout the state, and was on the planning committee for the Governor's Conference.

Cecil T. Young is past president of the Friends of the Minneapolis Public Library and has served on the board in a variety of positions. He served as a member of the interim board of Friends of Libraries USA and is a member of ALA's Friends of Libraries Committee.

Bibliography

HISTORY

American Library Association. Public Libraries Division. "Friends of Public Libraries: A Survey of Origins, Structures and Activities of Friends of the Library Groups." In S. Janice Kee and Dorothy K. Smith, eds., *Friends of Public Libraries: How They Work,* p.5-59. PLD Reporter, no. 3. Chicago: The Association, 1955.

"Friends." *American Libraries* 1:421, 637-38 (May 1970).

"Friends Are Money Raisers." *American Libraries* 5:231 (May 1974).

Gwyn, Ann; McArthur, Ann; and Furlow, Karen. "Friends of the Library." *College and Research Libraries* 36:272-82 (July 1975).

Hickey, Damon D. "The Friends of Duke University Library—A Short History." *Library Notes* 46:8-19 (Sept. 1976).

Hyde, Mary C. "History of Library Friends and the Phoenix Story of Columbia." *Columbia Library Columns* 20:3-15 (May 1971).

Leatherbury, Maurice C. *Friends of the Library Groups in Health Sciences Libraries.* Houston: Houston Academy of Medicine, Texas Medical Center, 1977.

Meyer, Leopold L. "Friends of the Library—Project of the University of Houston." In his *The Days of My Years: Autobiographical Reflections of Leopold L. Meyer,* p.97-100, 335-36. Houston: Leopold L. Meyer, 1975.

Mortenson, Cay. "Thoughts on Friends." *California Librarian* 27:33-36 (Jan. 1966).

O'Keefe, Richard L. "The Friends of the Fondren Library."
    Rice University Review, p.12-15 (Summer 1971).
Schreiber, Louis. "A Unique Friends of the Library Group."
    College and Research Libraries 16:365-67 (Oct. 1955).
Thorp, Willard. "The First Twenty-Five Years." *Princeton
    University Library Chronicle* 16:157-65 (Summer 1955).

SURVEYS

Bradshaw, Lillian Moore. "Friends of the Library." In *The
    Bowker Annual of Library and Book Trade Information,
    1968,* p.302-3. New York: Bowker, 1968.
Brewer, Frances J. "Friends of the Library and Other Bene-
    factors and Donors." *Library Trends* 9:453-65 (Apr.
    1961).
Butler, Catherine J., comp. *Friends of the Library Groups:
    Public Library Edition.* 4th ed. Chicago: American Li-
    brary Assn., 1951.
Dempsey, Frank J. "Friends of the Library." In *The Bowker
    Annual of Library and Book Trade Information, 1970,*
    p.355-56. New York: Bowker, 1970.
Dolnick, Sandy. "Friends of Libraries." In *The ALA Yearbook,*
    v.5. Chicago: American Library Assn., 1980.
Fox, M. Allyn. "Friends of the Library Groups in Colleges
    and Universities." *College and Research Libraries* 12:
    353-54 (Oct. 1951).
"Friends of the Library Organizations." *SPEC Flyer,* no. 6
    (Apr. 1974).
Shelley, Laura. "Friends of Libraries." In *The ALA Yearbook,*
    v.1-4. Chicago: American Library Assn., 1976-79.

MANUALS

Comingore, Gloria, and Petersen, Pat. *Book Sale Manual.* Tor-
    rance, California: Friends of the Torrance Library,
    1976.
Flanagan, Joan. *The Grass Roots Fundraising Book.* Chicago:
    Swallow, 1977.
Friends of California Libraries. *Information Kit.* Sierra
    Madre, California: Friends of California Libraries,
    1978.
Friends of Wisconsin Libraries. *Planning To Be Friends.*
    Pewaukee: Friends of Wisconsin Libraries, 1977.
Kee, S. Janice, and Smith, Dorothy K., eds. *Friends of Pub-
    lic Libraries: How They Work.* PLD Reporter, no. 3.
    Chicago: American Library Assn., 1955.
Moran, Irene, comp. *The Library Public Relations Recipe Book.*

Chicago: Public Relations Section, Library Administration Division, American Library Assn., 1978.

Pennell, H. Barrett, Jr. *Find Out Who Your Friends Are: (A Practical Manual for the Formation of Library Support Groups)*. Philadelphia: Friends of The Free Library of Philadelphia, 1978.

Sly, Janice Rae, and Childers, Louise, eds. *Friends of Florida's Public Libraries, A Practical Guide for Establishing and Maintaining an Effective Association*. Tallahassee: State Library of Florida, 1978.

Thompson, Lawrence S. "Friends of the Library." In *American Library and Book Trade Annual, 1959*, p.155-56. New York: Bowker, 1959.

Wallace, Sarah Leslie, ed. *Friends of the Library: Organization and Activities*. Chicago: American Library Assn., 1962.

LOBBYING AND FUNDRAISING

American Library Association. Legislation Committee. *Who Me? A Lobbyist?* Washington: The Association, 1976.

_____. Public Information Office. *A Perspective on Libraries: Facts, Figures, and Opinions about Libraries and Reading*. Chicago: The Association, 1979.

League of Women Voters Education Fund. *Anatomy of a Hearing: information on how to prepare for and conduct yourself at a hearing and how to request a hearing on a particular issue if none is scheduled*. Washington: League of Women Voters Education Fund, 1972. (Publication no. 108.)

_____. *Tell It to Washington*. Washington: League of Women Voters Education Fund, 1979. (Publication no. 349.)

New York Library Association. *The Library Lobbyist--A Guide to Action in the State Capitol*. Rev. ed. New York: The Association, 1977.

Seymour, Whitney North, Jr., and Layne, Elizabeth N. *For the People: Fighting for Public Libraries*. New York: Doubleday, 1979.

U. S. Department of the Treasury. Internal Revenue Service. *Lobbying of Eligible Public Charities*. Department of the Treasury, Internal Revenue Service, Notice 451, May 1977. (Excerpt from Publication 557.)

Weithorn, Stanley S. *Expanded Scope of Permissible Lobbying Activity Under the Tax Reform Act of 1976*. Special Memorandum prepared for members of the National Assembly of National Voluntary Health and Social Welfare Organizations, Inc. New York, 1979.

Winning the Money Game: A Guide to Community-Based Library Fundraising. New York: Baker and Taylor, 1979.

Index

Compiled by MARY HAMMEL DAVIS

Designed by Vladimir Reichl
Composed in IBM Selectric Orator and Courier
with Compugraphic Souvenir display type
by Vladimir Reichl & Associates
Printed on 50# Warren's 1854, a pH neutral stock,
and bound by Braun-Brumfield, Inc.